The Art of Readable Code

Dustin Boswell and Trevor Foucher

O'REILLY®

Beijing · Cambridge · Farnham · Köln · Sebastopol · Tokyo

The Art of Readable Code
by Dustin Boswell and Trevor Foucher

Published by O'Reilly Media, Inc., 1005 Gravenstein Highway North, Sebastopol, CA 95472.

O'Reilly books may be purchased for educational, business, or sales promotional use. Online editions are also available for most titles (*http://my.safaribooksonline.com*). For more information, contact our corporate/institutional sales department: (800) 998-9938 or *corporate@oreilly.com*.

Editor: Mary Treseler	**Indexer:** Potomac Indexing, LLC
Production Editor: Teresa Elsey	**Cover Designer:** Susan Thompson
Copyeditor: Nancy Wolfe Kotary	**Interior Designer:** David Futato
Proofreader: Teresa Elsey	**Illustrators:** Dave Allred and Robert Romano

November 2011:   First Edition.

Revision History for the First Edition:
    2011-11-01   First release
See *http://oreilly.com/catalog/errata.csp?isbn=9780596802295* for release details.

ISBN: 978-0-596-80229-5

[LSI]

1320155288

CONTENTS

PREFACE

We've worked at highly successful software companies, with outstanding engineers, and the code we encounter still has plenty of room for improvement. In fact, we've seen some really ugly code, and you probably have too.

But when we see beautifully written code, it's inspiring. Good code can teach you what's going on very quickly. It's fun to use, and it motivates you to make your own code better.

The goal of this book is help you make your code better. And when we say "code," we literally mean the lines of code you are staring at in your editor. We're not talking about the overall architecture of your project, or your choice of design patterns. Those are certainly important, but in our experience most of our day-to-day lives as programmers are spent on the "basic" stuff, like naming variables, writing loops, and attacking problems down at the function level. And a big part of this is reading and editing the code that's already there. We hope you'll find this book so helpful to your day-to-day programming that you'll recommend it to everyone on your team.

What This Book Is About

This book is about how to write code that's highly readable. The key idea in this book is that **code should be easy to understand**. Specifically, your goal should be to minimize the time it takes someone else to understand your code.

This book explains this idea and illustrates it with lots of examples from different languages, including C++, Python, JavaScript, and Java. We've avoided any advanced language features, so even if you don't know all these languages, it should still be easy to follow along. (In our experience, the concepts of readability are mostly language-independent, anyhow.)

Each chapter dives into a different aspect of coding and how to make it "easy to understand." The book is divided into four parts:

Surface-level improvements
> Naming, commenting, and aesthetics—simple tips that apply to every line of your codebase

Simplifying loops and logic
> Ways to refine the loops, logic, and variables in your program to make them easier to understand

Reorganizing your code
> Higher-level ways to organize large blocks of code and attack problems at the function level

Selected topics
> Applying "easy to understand" to testing and to a larger data structure coding example

How to Read This Book

Our book is intended to be a fun, casual read. We hope most readers will read the whole book in a week or two.

The chapters are ordered by "difficulty": basic topics are at the beginning, and more advanced topics are at the end. However, each chapter is self-contained and can be read in isolation. So feel free to skip around if you'd like.

Using Code Examples

This book is here to help you get your job done. In general, you may use the code in this book in your programs and documentation. You do not need to contact us for permission unless you're reproducing a significant portion of the code. For example, writing a program that uses several chunks of code from this book does not require permission. Selling or distributing a CD-ROM of examples from O'Reilly books does require permission. Answering a question by citing this book and quoting example code does not require permission. Incorporating a significant amount of example code from this book into your product's documentation does require permission.

We appreciate, but do not require, attribution. An attribution usually includes the title, author, publisher, and ISBN. For example: "*The Art of Readable Code* by Dustin Boswell and Trevor Foucher. Copyright 2012 Dustin Boswell and Trevor Foucher, 978-0-596-80229-5."

If you feel your use of code examples falls outside fair use or the permission given above, feel free to contact us at *permissions@oreilly.com*.

Safari® Books Online

 Safari Books Online is an on-demand digital library that lets you easily search over 7,500 technology and creative reference books and videos to find the answers you need quickly.

With a subscription, you can read any page and watch any video from our library online. Read books on your cell phone and mobile devices. Access new titles before they are available for print, and get exclusive access to manuscripts in development and post feedback for the authors. Copy and paste code samples, organize your favorites, download chapters, bookmark key sections, create notes, print out pages, and benefit from tons of other time-saving features.

O'Reilly Media has uploaded this book to the Safari Books Online service. To have full digital access to this book and others on similar topics from O'Reilly and other publishers, sign up for free at *http://my.safaribooksonline.com*.

How to Contact Us

Please address comments and questions concerning this book to the publisher:

O'Reilly Media, Inc.
1005 Gravenstein Highway North
Sebastopol, CA 95472
800-998-9938 (in the United States or Canada)
707-829-0515 (international or local)
707-829-0104 (fax)

We have a web page for this book, where we list errata, examples, and any additional information. You can access this page at:

http://shop.oreilly.com/product/9780596802301.do

To comment or ask technical questions about this book, send email to:

bookquestions@oreilly.com

For more information about our books, courses, conferences, and news, see our website at *http://www.oreilly.com.*

Find us on Facebook: *http://facebook.com/oreilly*

Follow us on Twitter: *http://twitter.com/oreillymedia*

Watch us on YouTube: *http://www.youtube.com/oreillymedia*

Acknowledgments

We'd like to thank our colleagues who donated their time to review our entire manuscript, including Alan Davidson, Josh Ehrlich, Rob Konigsberg, Archie Russell, Gabe W., and Asaph Zemach. Any errors in the book are entirely their fault (just kidding).

We're grateful to the many reviewers who gave us detailed feedback on various drafts of our book, including Michael Hunger, George Heineman, and Chuck Hudson.

We also got numerous ideas and feedback from John Blackburn, Tim Dasilva, Dennis Geels, Steve Gerding, Chris Harris, Josh Hyman, Joel Ingram, Erik Mavrinac, Greg Miller, Anatole Paine, and Nick White. Thanks to the numerous online commenters who reviewed our draft on O'Reilly's OFPS system.

Thanks to the team at O'Reilly for their endless patience and support, specifically Mary Treseler (editor), Teresa Elsey (production editor), Nancy Kotary (copyeditor), Rob Romano (illustrator), Jessica Hosman (tools), and Abby Fox (tools). And also to our cartoonist, Dave Allred, who made our crazy cartoon ideas come to life.

Lastly, we'd like to thank Melissa and Suzanne, for encouraging us along the way and putting up with incessant programming conversations.

## CHAPTER ONE

Code Should Be Easy to Understand

Over the past five years, we have collected hundreds of examples of "bad code" (much of it our own), and analyzed what made it bad, and what principles/techniques were used to make it better. What we noticed is that all of the principles stem from a single theme.

KEY IDEA
Code should be easy to understand.

We believe this is the most important guiding principle you can use when deciding how to write your code. Throughout the book, we'll show how to apply this principle to different aspects of your day-to-day coding. But before we begin, we'll elaborate on this principle and justify why it's so important.

What Makes Code "Better"?

Most programmers (including the authors) make programming decisions based on gut feel and intuition. We all know that code like this:

```
for (Node* node = list->head; node != NULL; node = node->next)
    Print(node->data);
```

is better than code like this:

```
Node* node = list->head;
if (node == NULL) return;

while (node->next != NULL) {
    Print(node->data);
    node = node->next;
}
if (node != NULL) Print(node->data);
```

(even though both examples behave exactly the same).

But a lot of times, it's a tougher choice. For example, is this code:

```
return exponent >= 0 ? mantissa * (1 << exponent) : mantissa / (1 << -exponent);
```

better or worse than:

```
if (exponent >= 0) {
    return mantissa * (1 << exponent);
} else {
    return mantissa / (1 << -exponent);
}
```

The first version is more compact, but the second version is less intimidating. Which criterion is more important? In general, how do you decide which way to code something?

CHAPTER TWO

Packing Information into Names

Whether you're naming a variable, a function, or a class, a lot of the same principles apply. We like to think of a name as a tiny comment. Even though there isn't much room, you can convey a lot of information by choosing a good name.

> **KEY IDEA**
>
> **Pack information into your names.**

A lot of the names we see in programs are vague, like tmp. Even words that may seem reasonable, such as size or get, don't pack much information. This chapter shows you how to pick names that do.

This chapter is organized into six specific topics:

- Choosing specific words
- Avoiding generic names (or knowing when to use them)
- Using concrete names instead of abstract names
- Attaching extra information to a name, by using a suffix or prefix
- Deciding how long a name should be
- Using name formatting to pack extra information

Choose Specific Words

Part of "packing information into names" is choosing words that are very specific and avoiding "empty" words.

For example, the word "get" is very unspecific, as in this example:

```
def GetPage(url):
    ...
```

The word "get" doesn't really say much. Does this method get a page from a local cache, from a database, or from the Internet? If it's from the Internet, a more specific name might be FetchPage() or DownloadPage().

Here's an example of a BinaryTree class:

```
class BinaryTree {
    int Size();
    ...
};
```

What would you expect the Size() method to return? The height of the tree, the number of nodes, or the memory footprint of the tree?

The problem is that Size() doesn't convey much information. A more specific name would be Height(), NumNodes(), or MemoryBytes().

But what if `--run_locally` needs to do more than just extra logging? For instance, suppose that it needs to set up and use a special local database. Now the name `--run_locally` seems more tempting because it can control both of these at once.

But using it for that purpose would be picking a name *because* it's vague and indirect, which is probably not a good idea. The better solution is to create a second flag named `--use_local_database`. Even though you have to use two flags now, these flags are much more explicit; they don't try to smash two orthogonal ideas into one, and they give you the option of using just one and not the other.

Attaching Extra Information to a Name

As we mentioned before, a variable's name is like a tiny comment. Even though there isn't much room, any extra information you squeeze into a name will be seen every time the variable is seen.

So if there's something very important about a variable that the reader must know, it's worth attaching an extra "word" to the name. For example, suppose you had a variable that contained a hexadecimal string:

```
string id;  // Example: "af84ef845cd8"
```

You might want to name it hex_id instead, if it's important for the reader to remember the ID's format.

Values with Units

If your variable is a measurement (such as an amount of time or a number of bytes), it's helpful to encode the units into the variable's name.

For example, here is some JavaScript code that measures the load time of a web page:

```
var start = (new Date()).getTime();  // top of the page
...
var elapsed = (new Date()).getTime() - start;  // bottom of the page
document.writeln("Load time was: " + elapsed + " seconds");
```

There is nothing obviously wrong with this code, but it doesn't work, because getTime() returns milliseconds, not seconds.

By appending _ms to our variables, we can make everything more explicit:

```
var start_ms = (new Date()).getTime();  // top of the page
...
var elapsed_ms = (new Date()).getTime() - start_ms;  // bottom of the page
document.writeln("Load time was: " + elapsed_ms / 1000 + " seconds");
```

Besides time, there are plenty of other units that come up in programming. Here is a table of unitless function parameters, and better versions that include the units:

Function parameter	Renaming parameter to encode units
Start(int **delay**)	delay → **delay_secs**
CreateCache(int **size**)	size → **size_mb**
ThrottleDownload(float **limit**)	limit → **max_kbps**
Rotate(float **angle**)	angle → **degrees_cw**

Encoding Other Important Attributes

This technique of attaching extra information to a name isn't limited to values with units. You should do it any time there's something dangerous or surprising about the variable.

Names That Can't Be Misconstrued

In the previous chapter, we covered how to put a lot of information into your names. In this chapter, we focus on a different topic: watching out for names that can be misunderstood.

> **KEY IDEA**
>
> **Actively scrutinize your names by asking yourself, "What other meanings could someone interpret from this name?"**

Really try to be creative here, actively seeking "wrong interpretations." This step will help you spot those ambiguous names so you can change them.

For the examples in this chapter, we're going to "think aloud" as we discuss the misinterpretations of each name we see, and then pick better names.

Example: Filter()

Suppose you're writing code to manipulate a set of database results:

```
results = Database.all_objects.filter("year <= 2011")
```

What does results now contain?

- Objects whose year is <= 2011?
- Objects whose year is *not* <= 2011?

The problem is that filter is an ambiguous word. It's unclear whether it means "to pick out" or "to get rid of." It's best to avoid the name filter because it's so easily misconstrued.

If you want "to pick out," a better name is select(). If you want "to get rid of," a better name is exclude().

Example: Clip(text, length)

Suppose you have a function that clips the contents of a paragraph:

```
# Cuts off the end of the text, and appends "..."
def Clip(text, length):
    ...
```

There are two ways you can imagine how Clip() behaves:

- It removes length from the end
- It truncates to a maximum length

The second way (truncation) is most likely, but you never know for sure. Rather than leave your reader with any nagging doubt, it would be better to name the function Truncate(text, length).

However, the parameter name `length` is also to blame. If it were `max_length`, that would make it even more clear.

But we're still not done. The name `max_length` still leaves multiple interpretations:

- A number of bytes
- A number of characters
- A number of words

As you saw in the previous chapter, this is a case where the units should be attached to the name. In this case, we mean "number of characters," so instead of `max_length`, it should be `max_chars`.

Prefer min and max for (Inclusive) Limits

Let's say your shopping cart application needs to stop people from buying more than 10 items at once:

```
CART_TOO_BIG_LIMIT = 10

if shopping_cart.num_items() >= CART_TOO_BIG_LIMIT:
    Error("Too many items in cart.")
```

This code has a classic off-by-one bug. We could easily fix it by changing `>=` to `>`:

```
if shopping_cart.num_items() > CART_TOO_BIG_LIMIT:
```

(or by redefining `CART_TOO_BIG_LIMIT` to 11). But the root problem is that `CART_TOO_BIG_LIMIT` is an ambiguous name—it's not clear whether you mean "up to" or "up to and including."

> **ADVICE**
>
> **The clearest way to name a limit is to put `max_` or `min_` in front of the thing being limited.**

In this case, the name should be `MAX_ITEMS_IN_CART`. The new code is simple and clear:

```
MAX_ITEMS_IN_CART = 10

if shopping_cart.num_items() > MAX_ITEMS_IN_CART:
    Error("Too many items in cart.")
```

Prefer first and last for Inclusive Ranges

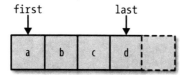

Here is another example where you can't tell if it's "up to" or "up to and including":

```
print integer_range(start=2, stop=4)
# Does this print [2,3] or [2,3,4] (or something else)?
```

Although start is a reasonable parameter name, stop can be interpreted in multiple ways here.

For *inclusive* ranges likes these (where the range should include both end points), a good choice is first/last. For instance:

```
set.PrintKeys(first="Bart", last="Maggie")
```

Unlike stop, the word last is clearly inclusive.

In addition to first/last, the names min/max may also work for inclusive ranges, assuming they "sound right" in that context.

Prefer begin and end for Inclusive/Exclusive Ranges

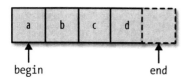

In practice, it's often more convenient to use inclusive/exclusive ranges. For example, if you want to print all the events that happened on October 16, it's easier to write:

```
PrintEventsInRange("OCT 16 12:00am", "OCT 17 12:00am")
```

than it is to write:

```
PrintEventsInRange("OCT 16 12:00am", "OCT 16 11:59:59.9999pm")
```

So what is a good pair of names for these parameters? Well, the typical programming convention for naming an inclusive/exclusive range is begin/end.

But the word end is a little ambiguous. For example, in the sentence, "I'm at the end of the book," the "end" is inclusive. Unfortunately, English doesn't have a succinct word for "just past the last value."

Because begin/end is so idiomatic (at least, it's used this way in the standard library for C++, and most places where an array needs to be "sliced" this way), it's the best option.

Naming Booleans

When picking a name for a boolean variable or a function that returns a boolean, be sure it's clear what true and false really mean.

Here's a dangerous example:

```
bool read_password = true;
```

Depending on how you read it (no pun intended), there are two very different interpretations:

- We *need* to read the password
- The password has already *been* read

In this case, it's best to avoid the word "read," and name it need_password or user_is_authenticated instead.

In general, adding words like is, has, can, or should can make booleans more clear.

For example, a function named SpaceLeft() sounds like it might return a number. If it were meant to return a boolean, a better name would be HasSpaceLeft().

Finally, it's best to avoid *negated* terms in a name. For example, instead of:

```
bool disable_ssl = false;
```

it would be easier to read (and more compact) to say:

```
bool use_ssl = true;
```

Matching Expectations of Users

Some names are misleading because the user has a preconceived idea of what the name means, even though you mean something else. In these cases, it's best to just "give in" and change the name so that it's not misleading.

Example: get*()

Many programmers are used to the convention that methods starting with get are "lightweight accessors" that simply return an internal member. Going against this convention is likely to mislead those users.

Here's an example, in Java, of what *not* to do:

```java
public class StatisticsCollector {
    public void addSample(double x) { ... }

    public double getMean() {
        // Iterate through all samples and return total / num_samples
    }
    ...
}
```

In this case, the implementation of getMean() is to iterate over past data and calculate the mean on the fly. This step might be very expensive if there's a lot of data! But an unsuspecting programmer might call getMean() carelessly, assuming that it's an inexpensive call.

Instead, the method should be renamed to something like computeMean(), which sounds more like an expensive operation. (Alternatively, it should be reimplemented to indeed be a lightweight operation.)

Example: list::size()

Here's an example from the C++ Standard Library. The following code was the cause of a very difficult-to-find bug that made one of our servers slow down to a crawl:

```cpp
void ShrinkList(list<Node>& list, int max_size) {
    while (list.size() > max_size) {
        FreeNode(list.back());
        list.pop_back();
    }
}
```

The "bug" is that the author didn't know that list.size() is an $O(n)$ operation—it counts through the linked list node by node, instead of just returning a precalculated count, which makes ShrinkList() an $O(n^2)$ operation.

The code is technically "correct," and in fact passed all our unit tests. But when ShrinkList() was called on a list with a million elements, it took over an hour to finish!

Maybe you're thinking, "That's the caller's fault—he or she should have read the documentation more carefully." That's true, but in this case, the fact that list.size() isn't a constant-time operation is *surprising*. All of the other containers in C++ have a constant-time size() method.

Had size() been named countSize() or countElements(), the same mistake would be less likely. The writers of the C++ Standard Library probably wanted to name the method size() to match all the other containers like vector and map. But because they did, programmers easily mistake it to be a fast operation, the way it is for other containers. Thankfully, the latest C++ standard now mandates size() to be $O(1)$.

Example: Evaluating Multiple Name Candidates

When deciding on a good name, you might have multiple candidates that you're considering. It's common to debate the merits of each name in your head before settling on the final choice. The following example illustrates this critiquing process.

High-traffic websites often use "experiments" to test whether a change to the website improves business. Here's an example of a config file that controls some experiments:

```
experiment_id: 100
description: "increase font size to 14pt"
traffic_fraction: 5%
...
```

Each experiment is defined by about 15 attribute/value pairs. Unfortunately, when defining another experiment that's very similar, you have to copy and paste most of those lines:

```
experiment_id: 101
description: "increase font size to 13pt"
[other lines identical to experiment_id 100]
```

Suppose we want to fix this situation by introducing a way to have one experiment reuse the properties from another. (This is the "prototype inheritance" pattern.) The end result is that you would type something like:

```
experiment_id: 101
the_other_experiment_id_I_want_to_reuse: 100
[change any properties as needed]
```

The question is: what should the_other_experiment_id_I_want_to_reuse really be named?

Here are four names to consider:

1. template
2. reuse
3. copy
4. inherit

Any of these names make sense to *us* because we're the ones adding this new feature to the config language. But we have to imagine how the name will sound to someone who comes across the code and doesn't know about this feature. So let's analyze each name, thinking of ways someone could misinterpret it.

1. Let's imagine using the name template:

```
experiment_id: 101
template: 100
...
```

template has a couple problems. First, it's not clear whether it's saying "I am a template" or "I am using this other template." Second, a "template" is often something *abstract* that must be "filled in" before it is *concrete*. Someone might think a templated experiment isn't a "real" experiment. Overall, template is just too vague in this situation.

2. How about reuse:

```
experiment_id: 101
reuse: 100
...
```

reuse is an okay word, but as written, someone might think it's saying, "This experiment can be reused at most 100 times." Changing the name to reuse_id would help. But a confused reader might think reuse_id: 100 means "my id for reuse is 100."

3. Let's consider copy.

```
experiment_id: 101
copy: 100
...
```

copy is a good word. But by itself, copy: 100 seems like it might be saying "copy this experiment 100 times" or "this is the 100th copy of something." To make it clear that this term refers to *another* experiment, we could change the name to copy_experiment. This is probably the best name so far.

4. But now let's consider inherit:

```
experiment_id: 101
inherit: 100
...
```

The word "inherit" is familiar to most programmers, and it's understood that further modifications are made after inheritance. With class inheritance, you get all the methods and members of another class and then modify them or add more. Even in real life, when you inherit possessions from a relative, it's understood that you might sell them or own other things yourself.

But again, let's make it clear that we're inheriting from another experiment. We can improve the name to inherit_from or even inherit_from_experiment_id.

Overall, `copy_experiment` and `inherit_from_experiment_id` are the best names, because they most clearly describe what's happening and are least likely to be misunderstood.

Summary

The best names are ones that can't be misconstrued—the person reading your code will understand it the way you meant it, and no other way. Unfortunately, a lot of English words are ambiguous when it comes to programming, such as `filter`, `length`, and `limit`.

Before you decide on a name, play devil's advocate and imagine how your name might be misunderstood. The best names are resistant to misinterpretation.

When it comes to defining an upper or lower limit for a value, `max_` and `min_` are good prefixes to use. For inclusive ranges, `first` and `last` are good. For inclusive/exclusive ranges, `begin` and `end` are best because they're the most idiomatic.

When naming a boolean, use words like `is` and `has` to make it clear that it's a boolean. Avoid negated terms (e.g., `disable_ssl`).

Beware of users' expectations about certain words. For example, users may expect `get()` or `size()` to be lightweight methods.

## CHAPTER FOUR

Aesthetics

A lot of thought goes into the layout of a magazine—the length of the paragraphs, the width of the columns, the order of the articles, and what goes on the cover. A good magazine makes it easy to skip around from page to page, but also easy to read straight through.

Good source code should be just as "easy on the eyes." In this chapter, we'll show how good use of spacing, alignment, and ordering can make your code easier to read.

Specifically, there are three principles we use:

- Use consistent layout, with patterns the reader can get used to.
- Make similar code look similar.
- Group related lines of code into blocks.

AESTHETICS VS. DESIGN

In this chapter, we're concerned only with simple "aesthetic" improvements you can make to your code. These types of changes are easy to make and often improve readability quite a bit. There are times when larger refactoring of your code (such as splitting out new functions or classes) can help even more. Our view is that good aesthetics and good design are independent ideas; ideally you should strive for both.

Why Do Aesthetics Matter?

```
email    = request.POST.get('email')
url      = request.POST.get('url')
```

As you may have noticed, the third definition has a typo (equest instead of request). Mistakes like these are more pronounced when everything is lined up so neatly.

In the wget codebase, the available command-line options (more than 100 of them) were listed as follows:

```
commands[] = {
    ...
    { "timeout",       NULL,                cmd_spec_timeout },
    { "timestamping",  &opt.timestamping,   cmd_boolean },
    { "tries",         &opt.ntry,           cmd_number_inf },
    { "useproxy",      &opt.use_proxy,      cmd_boolean },
    { "useragent",     NULL,                cmd_spec_useragent },
    ...
};
```

This approach made the list very easy to skim through and jump from one column to the next.

Should You Use Column Alignment?

Column edges provide "visual handrails" that make it easier to scan through. It's a good example of "make similar code look similar."

But some programmers don't like it. One reason is that it takes more work to set up and maintain the alignment. Another reason is it creates a larger "diff" when making changes—a one-line change might cause five other lines to change (mostly just whitespace).

Our advice is to try it. In our experience, it doesn't take as much work as programmers fear. And if it does, you can simply stop.

Pick a Meaningful Order, and Use It Consistently

There are many cases where the order of code doesn't affect the correctness. For instance, these five variable definitions could be written in any order:

```
details  = request.POST.get('details')
location = request.POST.get('location')
phone    = request.POST.get('phone')
email    = request.POST.get('email')
url      = request.POST.get('url')
```

In situations like this, it's helpful to put them in some meaningful order, not just random. Here are some ideas:

- Match the order of the variables to the order of the <input> fields on the corresponding HTML form.

- Order them from "most important" to "least important."
- Order them alphabetically.

Whatever the order, you should use the same order throughout your code. It would be confusing to change the order later on:

```
if details:  rec.details  = details
if phone:    rec.phone    = phone      # Hey, where did 'location' go?
if email:    rec.email    = email
if url:      rec.url      = url
if location: rec.location = location   # Why is 'location' down here now?
```

Organize Declarations into Blocks

The brain naturally thinks in terms of groups and hierarchies, so you can help a reader quickly digest your code by organizing it that way.

For example, here's a C++ class for a frontend server, with all its method declarations:

```
class FrontendServer {
  public:
    FrontendServer();
    void ViewProfile(HttpRequest* request);
    void OpenDatabase(string location, string user);
    void SaveProfile(HttpRequest* request);
    string ExtractQueryParam(HttpRequest* request, string param);
    void ReplyOK(HttpRequest* request, string html);
    void FindFriends(HttpRequest* request);
    void ReplyNotFound(HttpRequest* request, string error);
    void CloseDatabase(string location);
    ~FrontendServer();
};
```

This code isn't horrible, but the layout certainly doesn't help the reader digest all those methods. Instead of listing all the methods in one giant block, they should be logically organized into groups, like this:

```
class FrontendServer {
  public:
    FrontendServer();
    ~FrontendServer();

    // Handlers
    void ViewProfile(HttpRequest* request);
    void SaveProfile(HttpRequest* request);
    void FindFriends(HttpRequest* request);

    // Request/Reply Utilities
    string ExtractQueryParam(HttpRequest* request, string param);
    void ReplyOK(HttpRequest* request, string html);
    void ReplyNotFound(HttpRequest* request, string error);
```

```
    // Database Helpers
    void OpenDatabase(string location, string user);
    void CloseDatabase(string location);
};
```

This version is much easier to digest. It's also easier to read, even though there are more lines of code. The reason is that you can quickly figure out the four high-level sections and then read the details of each section when it's necessary.

Break Code into "Paragraphs"

Written text is broken into paragraphs for a number of reasons:

- It's a way to group similar ideas together and set them apart from other ideas.

- It provides a visual "stepping stone"—without it, it's easy to lose your place on the page.

- It facilitates navigation from one paragraph to another.

Code should be broken into "paragraphs" for the same reasons. For example, no one likes to read a giant lump of code like this:

```
# Import the user's email contacts, and match them to users in our system.
# Then display a list of those users that he/she isn't already friends with.
def suggest_new_friends(user, email_password):
    friends = user.friends()
    friend_emails = set(f.email for f in friends)
    contacts = import_contacts(user.email, email_password)
    contact_emails = set(c.email for c in contacts)
    non_friend_emails = contact_emails - friend_emails
    suggested_friends = User.objects.select(email__in=non_friend_emails)
    display['user'] = user
    display['friends'] = friends
    display['suggested_friends'] = suggested_friends
    return render("suggested_friends.html", display)
```

It may not be obvious, but this function goes through a number of distinct steps. So it would be especially useful to break up those lines of code into paragraphs:

```
def suggest_new_friends(user, email_password):
    # Get the user's friends' email addresses.
    friends = user.friends()
    friend_emails = set(f.email for f in friends)

    # Import all email addresses from this user's email account.
    contacts = import_contacts(user.email, email_password)
    contact_emails = set(c.email for c in contacts)

    # Find matching users that they aren't already friends with.
    non_friend_emails = contact_emails - friend_emails
    suggested_friends = User.objects.select(email__in=non_friend_emails)
```

```
# Display these lists on the page.
display['user'] = user
display['friends'] = friends
display['suggested_friends'] = suggested_friends

return render("suggested_friends.html", display)
```

Notice that we also added a summary comment to each paragraph, which also helps the reader skim through the code. (See Chapter 5, *Knowing What to Comment.*)

As with written text, there may be multiple ways to break the code up, and programmers may prefer longer or shorter paragraphs.

Personal Style versus Consistency

There are certain aesthetic choices that just boil down to personal style. For instance, where the open brace for a class definition should go:

```
class Logger {
    ...
};
```

or

```
class Logger
{
    ...
};
```

If one of these styles is chosen over the other, it doesn't substantially affect the readability of the codebase. But if these two styles are mixed throughout the code, it does affect the readability.

We've worked on many projects where we felt like the team was using the "wrong" style, but we followed the project conventions because we knew that consistency is far more important.

> **KEY IDEA**
> **Consistent style is more important than the "right" style.**

Summary

Everyone prefers to read code that's aesthetically pleasing. By "formatting" your code in a consistent, meaningful way, you make it easier and faster to read.

Here are specific techniques we discussed:

- If multiple blocks of code are doing similar things, try to give them the same silhouette.
- Aligning parts of the code into "columns" can make code easy to skim through.
- If code mentions A, B, and C in one place, don't say B, C, and A in another. Pick a meaningful order and stick with it.
- Use empty lines to break apart large blocks into logical "paragraphs."

## CHAPTER FIVE

Knowing What to Comment

The goal of this chapter is to help you realize what you should be commenting. You might think the purpose of commenting is to "explain what the code does," but that is just a small part of it.

KEY IDEA

The purpose of commenting is to help the reader know as much as the writer did.

When you're writing code, you have a lot of valuable information in your head. When other people read your code, that information is lost—all they have is the code in front of them.

In this chapter, we'll show you many examples of when to write down that information in your head. We've left out the more mundane points about commenting; instead, we've focused on the more interesting and "underserved" aspects of commenting.

We've organized the chapter into the following areas:

- Knowing what *not* to comment
- Recording your thoughts as you code
- Putting yourself in the readers' shoes, to imagine what they'll need to know

What NOT to Comment

Reading a comment takes time away from reading the actual code, and each comment takes up space on the screen. That is, it better be worth it. So where do you draw the line between a worthless comment and a good one?

All of the comments in this code are worthless:

```
// The class definition for Account
class Account {
  public:
    // Constructor
    Account();

    // Set the profit member to a new value
    void SetProfit(double profit);

    // Return the profit from this Account
    double GetProfit();
};
```

These comments are worthless because they don't provide any new information or help the reader understand the code better.

KEY IDEA

Don't comment on facts that can be derived quickly from the code itself.

The word "quickly" is an important distinction, though. Consider the comment for this Python code:

```python
# remove everything after the second '*'
name = '*'.join(line.split('*')[:2])
```

Technically, this comment doesn't present any "new information" either. If you look at the code itself, you'll eventually figure out what it's doing. But for most programmers, reading the commented code is much faster than understanding the code without it.

Don't Comment Just for the Sake of Commenting

Some professors require their students to have a comment for each function in their homework code. As a result, some programmers feel guilty about leaving a function naked without comments and end up rewriting the function's name and arguments in sentence form:

```cpp
// Find the Node in the given subtree, with the given name, using the given depth.
Node* FindNodeInSubtree(Node* subtree, string name, int depth);
```

This one falls into the "worthless comments" category—the function's declaration and the comment are virtually the same. This comment should be either removed or improved.

If you want to have a comment here, it might as well elaborate on more important details:

```
// Find a Node with the given 'name' or return NULL.
// If depth <= 0, only 'subtree' is inspected.
// If depth == N, only 'subtree' and N levels below are inspected.
Node* FindNodeInSubtree(Node* subtree, string name, int depth);
```

Don't Comment Bad Names—Fix the Names Instead

A comment shouldn't have to make up for a bad name. For example, here's an innocent-looking comment for a function named CleanReply():

```
// Enforce limits on the Reply as stated in the Request,
// such as the number of items returned, or total byte size, etc.
void CleanReply(Request request, Reply reply);
```

Most of the comment is simply explaining what "clean" means. Instead, the phrase "enforce limits" should be moved into the function name:

```
// Make sure 'reply' meets the count/byte/etc. limits from the 'request'
void EnforceLimitsFromRequest(Request request, Reply reply);
```

This function name is more "self-documenting." A good name is better than a good comment because it will be seen everywhere the function is used.

Here is another example of a comment for a poorly named function:

```
// Releases the handle for this key. This doesn't modify the actual registry.
void DeleteRegistry(RegistryKey* key);
```

The name DeleteRegistry() sounds like a dangerous function (it *deletes* the registry?!). The comment "This doesn't modify the actual registry" is trying to clear up the confusion.

Instead, we could use a more self-documenting name like:

```
void ReleaseRegistryHandle(RegistryKey* key);
```

In general, you don't want "crutch comments"—comments that are trying to make up for the unreadability of the code. Coders often state this rule as **good code > bad code + good comments.**

Recording Your Thoughts

Now that you know what *not* to comment, let's discuss what *should* be commented (but often isn't).

A lot of good comments can come out of simply "recording your thoughts"—that is, the important thoughts you had as you were writing the code.

Include "Director Commentary"

Movies often have a "director commentary" track where the filmmakers give their insights and tell stories to help you understand how the film was made. Similarly, you should include comments to record valuable insights about the code.

Here's an example:

```
// Surprisingly, a binary tree was 40% faster than a hash table for this data.
// The cost of computing a hash was more than the left/right comparisons.
```

This comment teaches the reader something and stops any would-be optimizer from wasting their time.

Here's another example:

```
// This heuristic might miss a few words. That's OK; solving this 100% is hard.
```

Without this comment, the reader might think there's a bug and might waste time trying to come up with test cases that make it fail, or go off and try to fix the bug.

A comment can also explain why the code isn't in great shape:

```
// This class is getting messy. Maybe we should create a 'ResourceNode' subclass to
// help organize things.
```

This comment acknowledges that the code is messy but also encourages the next person to fix it (with specifics on how to get started). Without the comment, many readers would be intimidated by the messy code and afraid to touch it.

Comment the Flaws in Your Code

Code is constantly evolving and is bound to have flaws along the way. Don't be embarrassed to document those flaws. For example, noting when improvements should be made:

```
// TODO: use a faster algorithm
```

or when code is incomplete:

```
// TODO(dustin): handle other image formats besides JPEG
```

There are a number of markers that have become popular among programmers:

Marker	Typical meaning
TODO:	Stuff I haven't gotten around to yet
FIXME:	Known-broken code here
HACK:	Admittedly inelegant solution to a problem
XXX:	Danger! major problem here

Advertising Likely Pitfalls

When documenting a function or class, a good question to ask yourself is, *What is surprising about this code? How might it be misused?* Basically, you want to "think ahead" and anticipate the problems that people might run into when using your code.

For example, suppose you wrote a function that sends an email to a given user:

```
void SendEmail(string to, string subject, string body);
```

The implementation of this function involves connecting to an external email service, which might take up to a whole second, or possibly longer. Someone who is writing a web application might not realize this and mistakenly call this function while handling an HTTP request. (Doing this would cause their web application to "hang" if the email service is down.)

To prevent this likely mishap, you should comment on this "implementation detail":

```
// Calls an external service to deliver email.  (Times out after 1 minute.)
void SendEmail(string to, string subject, string body);
```

Here is another example: suppose you have a FixBrokenHtml() function that attempts to rewrite broken HTML by inserting missing closing tags and the like:

```
def FixBrokenHtml(html): ...
```

The function works great, except for the caveat that its running time blows up when there are deeply nested and unmatched tags. For nasty HTML inputs, this function could take *minutes* to execute.

Rather than let the user discover this later on his own, it's better to announce this upfront:

```
// Runtime is O(number_tags * average_tag_depth), so watch out for badly nested inputs.
def FixBrokenHtml(html): ...
```

"Big Picture" Comments

One of the hardest things for a new team member to understand is the "big picture"—how classes interact, how data flows through the whole system, and where the entry points are. The person who designed the system often forgets to comment about this stuff because he's so intimately involved with it.

Consider this thought experiment: **someone new just joined your team, she's sitting next to you, and you need to get her familiar with the codebase.**

As you're giving her a tour of the codebase, you might point out certain files or classes and say things like:

- "This is the glue code between our business logic and the database. None of the application code should use this directly."

- "This class looks complicated, but it's really just a smart cache. It doesn't know anything about the rest of the system."

After a minute of casual conversation, your new team member will know much more than she would from reading the source by herself.

This is exactly the type of information that should be included as high-level comments.

Here's a simple example of a file-level comment:

```
// This file contains helper functions that provide a more convenient interface to our
// file system. It handles file permissions and other nitty-gritty details.
```

Don't get overwhelmed by the thought that you have to write extensive, formal documentation. **A few well-chosen sentences are better than nothing at all.**

Summary Comments

Even deep inside a function, it's a good idea to comment on the "bigger picture." Here's an example of a comment that neatly summarizes the low-level code below it:

```
# Find all the items that customers purchased for themselves.
for customer_id in all_customers:
    for sale in all_sales[customer_id].sales:
        if sale.recipient == customer_id:
            ...
```

Without this comment, reading each line of code is a bit of a mystery. ("I see we're iterating through all_customers ... but what for?")

It's especially helpful to have these summary comments in longer functions where there are a few large "chunks" inside:

```
def GenerateUserReport():
    # Acquire a lock for this user
    ...

    # Read user's info from the database
    ...

    # Write info to a file
    ...

    # Release the lock for this user
```

These comments also act as a bulleted summary of what the function does, so the reader can get the gist of what the function does before diving into details. (If these chunks are easily separable, you might just make them functions of their own. As we mentioned before, good code is better than bad code with good comments.)

SHOULD YOU COMMENT THE WHAT, THE WHY, OR THE HOW?

You may have heard advice like, "Comment the *why*, not the *what* (or the how)." Although catchy, we feel these statements are too simplistic and mean different things to different people.

Our advice is to do whatever helps the reader understand the code more easily. This may involve commenting the *what*, the *how*, or the *why* (or all three).

Final Thoughts—Getting Over Writer's Block

A lot of coders don't like to write comments because it feels like a lot of work to write a good one. When writers have this sort of "writer's block," the best solution is to just start writing. So the next time you're hesitating to write a comment, just go ahead and comment what you're thinking, however half-baked it may be.

For example, suppose you're working on a function and think to yourself, *Oh crap, this stuff will get tricky if there are ever duplicates in this list.* Just write that down:

```
// Oh crap, this stuff will get tricky if there are ever duplicates in this list.
```

See, was that so hard? It's actually not that bad of a comment—certainly better than nothing. The language is a little vague though. To fix it, we can just go through each phrase and replace it with something more specific:

- By "oh crap," you really mean "Careful: this is something to watch out for."
- By "this stuff," you mean "the code that's handling this input."
- By "will get tricky," you mean "will be hard to implement."

The new comment might be:

```
// Careful: this code doesn't handle duplicates in the list (because that's hard to do)
```

Notice that we've broken down the task of writing a comment into these simpler steps:

1. Write down whatever comment is on your mind.
2. Read the comment, and see what (if anything) needs to be improved.
3. Make improvements.

As you comment more often, you'll find that the quality of comments from step 1 gets better and better and eventually might not need fixing at all. And by commenting early and often, you avoid the unpleasant situation of needing to write a bunch of comments at the end.

Summary

The purpose of a comment is to help the reader know what the writer knew when writing the code. This whole chapter is about realizing all the not-so-obvious nuggets of information you have about the code and writing those down.

What *not* to comment:

- Facts that can be quickly derived from the code itself.
- "Crutch comments" that make up for bad code (such as a bad function name)—fix the code instead.

Thoughts you should be recording include:

- Insights about why code is one way and not another ("director commentary").
- Flaws in your code, by using markers like TODO: or XXX:.
- The "story" for how a constant got its value.

Put yourself in the reader's shoes:

- Anticipate which parts of your code will make readers say "Huh?" and comment those.
- Document any surprising behavior an average reader wouldn't expect.
- Use "big picture" comments at the file/class level to explain how all the pieces fit together.
- Summarize blocks of code with comments so that the reader doesn't get lost in the details.

## CHAPTER SIX

Making Comments Precise and Compact

The previous chapter was about realizing *what* you should be commenting. This chapter is about *how* to write comments that are precise and compact.

If you're going to write a comment at all, it might as well be *precise*—as specific and detailed as possible. On the other hand, comments take up extra space on the screen, and take extra time to read. So comments should also be *compact*.

> ### KEY IDEA
> **Comments should have a high information-to-space ratio.**

The rest of the chapter shows examples of how to do this.

Keep Comments Compact

Here's an example of a comment for a C++ type definition:

```
// The int is the CategoryType.
// The first float in the inner pair is the 'score',
// the second is the 'weight'.
typedef hash_map<int, pair<float, float> > ScoreMap;
```

But why use three lines to explain it, when you can illustrate it in just one line?

```
// CategoryType -> (score, weight)
typedef hash_map<int, pair<float, float> > ScoreMap;
```

Some comments need three lines of space, but this is not one of them.

Avoid Ambiguous Pronouns

As the classic "Who's on First?" skit illustrated, pronouns can make things very confusing.

It takes extra work for the reader to "resolve" a pronoun. And in some cases, it's unclear what "it" or "this" is referring to. Here's an example:

```
// Insert the data into the cache, but check if it's too big first.
```

In this comment, "it" might refer to the data or the cache. You could probably figure that out by reading the rest of the code. But if you have to do that, what's the point of the comment?

The safest thing is to "fill in" pronouns if there's any chance of confusion. In the previous example, let's assume "it" was "the data":

```
// Insert the data into the cache, but check if the data is too big first.
```

This is the simplest change to make. You could also have restructured the sentence to make "it" perfectly clear:

```
// If the data is small enough, insert it into the cache.
```

Polish Sloppy Sentences

In many cases, making a comment more precise goes hand-in-hand with making it more compact.

Here is an example from a web crawler:

```
# Depending on whether we've already crawled this URL before, give it a different priority.
```

This sentence might seem okay, but compare it to this version:

```
# Give higher priority to URLs we've never crawled before.
```

This sentence is simpler, smaller, and more direct. It also explains that *higher* priority is given to uncrawled URLs—the previous comment didn't contain that information.

Describe Function Behavior Precisely

Imagine you just wrote a function that counts the number of lines in a file:

```
// Return the number of lines in this file.
int CountLines(string filename) { ... }
```

This comment isn't very precise—there are a lot of ways to define a "line." Here are some corner cases to think about:

- "" (an empty file)—0 or 1 line?
- "hello"—0 or 1 line?
- "hello\n"—1 or 2 lines?
- "hello\n world"—1 or 2 lines?
- "hello\n\r cruel\n world\r"—2, 3, or 4 lines?

The simplest implementation is to count the number of newline (\n) characters. (This is the way the Unix command wc works.) Here's a better comment to match this implementation:

```
// Count how many newline bytes ('\n') are in the file.
int CountLines(string filename) { ... }
```

This comment isn't much longer than the first version, but contains much more information. It tells the reader that the function might return 0 if there are no newlines. It also tells the reader that carriage returns (\r) are ignored.

Use Input/Output Examples That Illustrate Corner Cases

When it comes to comments, a carefully chosen input/output example can be worth a thousand words.

For example, here's a common function that removes parts of a string:

```
// Remove the suffix/prefix of 'chars' from the input 'src'.
String Strip(String src, String chars) { ... }
```

This comment isn't very precise because it can't answer questions such as:

- Is chars a whole substring that is to be removed, or effectively just an unordered set of letters?
- What if there are multiples of chars on the end of src?

Instead, a well-chosen example can answer these questions:

```
// ...
// Example: Strip("abba/a/ba", "ab") returns "/a/"
String Strip(String src, String chars) { ... }
```

The example "shows off" the full functionality of Strip(). Note that a simpler example wouldn't be as useful, if it doesn't answer those questions:

```
// Example: Strip("ab", "a") returns "b"
```

Here's another example of a function that could use an illustration:

```
// Rearrange 'v' so that elements < pivot come before those >= pivot;
// Then return the largest 'i' for which v[i] < pivot (or -1 if none are < pivot)
int Partition(vector<int>* v, int pivot);
```

This comment is actually very precise, but a little bit hard to visualize. Here's an example you could include to illustrate things further:

```
// ...
// Example: Partition([8 5 9 8 2], 8) might result in [5 2 | 8 9 8] and return 1
int Partition(vector<int>* v, int pivot);
```

There are a number of points to mention about the specific example input/output we chose:

- The pivot is equal to elements in the vector to illustrate that edge case.
- We put duplicates in the vector (8) to illustrate that this is an acceptable input.
- The resulting vector is not sorted—if it were, the reader might get the wrong idea.
- Because the return value was 1, we made sure 1 wasn't also a value in the vector—that would be confusing.

State the Intent of Your Code

As we mentioned in the previous chapter, commenting is often about telling the reader what you were thinking about when you wrote the code. Unfortunately, many comments end up just describing what the code does in literal terms, without adding much new information.

Here's an example of such a comment:

```
void DisplayProducts(list<Product> products) {
    products.sort(CompareProductByPrice);

    // Iterate through the list in reverse order
    for (list<Product>::reverse_iterator it = products.rbegin(); it != products.rend();
         ++it)
        DisplayPrice(it->price);

    ...
}
```

All this comment does is just describe the line below it. Instead, consider this better comment:

```
    // Display each price, from highest to lowest
    for (list<Product>::reverse_iterator it = products.rbegin(); ... )
```

This comment explains what the program is doing at a higher level. This is much more in tune with what the programmer was thinking when she wrote the code.

Interestingly, there is a bug in this program! The CompareProductByPrice function (not shown) already sorts higher-priced items first. The code is doing the opposite of what the author intended.

This is a good reason why the second comment is better. Despite the bug, the first comment is technically correct (the loop does iterate in reverse order). But with the second comment, a reader is more likely to notice that the intent of the writer (to show higher-priced items first) contradicts what the code actually does. In effect, the comment acts as a *redundancy check*.

Ultimately, the best redundancy check is a unit test (see Chapter 14, *Testing and Readability*). But it's still worthwhile having comments like these explaining the intent of your program.

"Named Function Parameter" Comments

Suppose you saw a function call like this one:

```
Connect(10, false);
```

This function call is a bit mysterious because of those integer and boolean literals being passed in.

In languages like Python, you can assign the arguments by name:

```
def Connect(timeout, use_encryption):  ...

# Call the function using named parameters
Connect(timeout = 10, use_encryption = False)
```

In languages like C++ and Java, you can't do this. However, you can use an inline comment to the same effect:

```
void Connect(int timeout, bool use_encryption) { ... }

// Call the function with commented parameters
Connect(/* timeout_ms = */ 10, /* use_encryption = */ false);
```

Notice that we "named" the first parameter timeout_ms instead of timeout. Ideally, the function's real argument would have been timeout_ms, but if for some reason we can't make this change, this is a handy way to "improve" the name.

When it comes to boolean arguments, it's especially important to put /* name = */ in *front* of the value. Putting the comment *behind* the value is very confusing:

```
// Don't do this!
Connect( ... , false /* use_encryption */);

// Don't do this either!
Connect( ... , false /* = use_encryption */);
```

In these examples, it's unclear whether false means "use encryption" or "don't use encryption".

Most function calls don't need comments like these, but it's a handy (and compact) way to explain mysterious-looking arguments.

Use Information-Dense Words

Once you've been programming for a number of years, you notice that the same general problems and solutions come up repeatedly. Often, there are specific words or phrases that have been developed to describe these patterns/idioms. Using these words can make your comments much more compact.

For example, suppose your comment were:

```
// This class contains a number of members that store the same information as in the
// database, but are stored here for speed. When this class is read from later, those
// members are checked first to see if they exist, and if so are returned; otherwise the
// database is read from and that data stored in those fields for next time.
```

Instead, you could just say:

```
// This class acts as a caching layer to the database.
```

As another example, a comment such as:

```
// Remove excess whitespace from the street address, and do lots of other cleanup
// like turn "Avenue" into "Ave." This way, if there are two different street addresses
// that are typed in slightly differently, they will have the same cleaned-up version and
// we can detect that these are equal.
```

could instead be:

```
// Canonicalize the street address (remove extra spaces, "Avenue" -> "Ave.", etc.)
```
There are lots of words and phrases that pack a lot of meaning, such as "heuristic," "brute-force," "naive solution," and the like. If you have a comment that feels a bit long-winded, see if it can be described as a typical programming situation.

Summary

This chapter is about writing comments that pack as much information into as small a space as possible. Here are the specific tips:

- Avoid pronouns like "it" and "this" when they can refer to multiple things.
- Describe a function's behavior with as much precision as is practical.
- Illustrate your comments with carefully chosen input/output examples.
- State the high-level intent of your code, rather than the obvious details.
- Use inline comments (e.g., Function(/* arg = */ ...)) to explain mysterious function arguments.
- Keep your comments brief by using words that pack a lot of meaning.

## PART II

Simplifying Loops and Logic

In Part I, we covered surface-level improvements—simple ways to improve the readability of your code one line at a time that can be applied without much risk or effort.

In this next part, we go deeper and discuss the "loops and logic" of your program: the control flow, logical expressions, and variables that make your code work. As always, our goal is to make these parts of your code easy to understand.

We do this by trying to minimize the "mental baggage" of your code. Every time you see a complicated loop, a giant expression, or a large number of variables, this adds to the mental baggage in your head. It requires you to think harder and remember more. This is exactly the opposite of "easy to understand." When code has a lot of mental baggage, bugs are more likely to go unnoticed, the code becomes harder to change, and it's just less fun to work with.

## CHAPTER SEVEN

Making Control Flow Easy to Read

If code had no conditionals, loops, or any other *control flow* statements, it would be very easy to read. These jumps and branches are the hard stuff, where code can get confusing quickly. This chapter is about making the control flow in your code easy to read.

> **KEY IDEA**
>
> **Make all your conditionals, loops, and other changes to control flow as "natural" as possible—written in a way that doesn't make the reader stop and reread your code.**

The Order of Arguments in Conditionals

Which of these two pieces of code is more readable:

```
if (length >= 10)
```

or

```
if (10 <= length)
```

To most programmers, the first is much more readable. But what about the next two:

```
while (bytes_received < bytes_expected)
```

or

```
while (bytes_expected > bytes_received)
```

Again, the first version is more readable. But why? What's the general rule? How do you decide whether it's better to write a < b or b > a?

Here's a guideline we've found useful:

Left-hand side	Right-hand side
The expression "being interrogated," whose value is more in flux.	The expression being compared against, whose value is more constant.

This guideline matches English usage—it's pretty natural to say, "if you make at least $100K/year" or "if you are at least 18 years old." It's unnatural to say, "if 18 years is less than or equal to your age."

This explains why while (bytes_received < bytes_expected) is more readable. bytes_received is the value that we're checking up on, and it's increasing as the loop executes. bytes_expected is the more "stable" value being compared against.

The Order of if/else Blocks

"CLASS, FIRST LET'S GIVE OUR UNDIVIDED ATTENTION TO BOBBY WHILE HE TALKS ABOUT HIS PET FROG!"

When writing an if/else statement, you usually have the freedom to swap the order of the blocks. For instance, you can either write it like:

```
if (a == b) {
    // Case One ...
} else {
    // Case Two ...
}
```

or as:

```
if (a != b) {
    // Case Two ...
} else {
    // Case One ...
}
```

You may not have given much thought about this before, but in some cases there are good reasons to prefer one order over the other:

- Prefer dealing with the *positive* case first instead of the negative—e.g., if (debug) instead of if (!debug).

- Prefer dealing with the *simpler* case first to get it out of the way. This approach might also allow both the if and the else to be visible on the screen at the same time, which is nice.

- Prefer dealing with the more *interesting* or conspicuous case first.

Sometimes these preferences conflict, and you have to make a judgment call. But in many cases, there is a clear winner.

For example, suppose you have a web server that's building a response based on whether the URL contains the query parameter expand_all:

```
if (!url.HasQueryParameter("expand_all")) {
    response.Render(items);
    ...
} else {
    for (int i = 0; i < items.size(); i++) {
        items[i].Expand();
    }
    ...
}
```

When the reader glances at the first line, her brain immediately thinks about the expand_all case. It's like when someone says, "Don't think of a pink elephant." You can't help but think about it—the "don't" is drowned out by the more unusual "pink elephant."

Here, expand_all is our pink elephant. Because it's the more interesting case (and it's the positive case, too), let's deal with it first:

```
if (url.HasQueryParameter("expand_all")) {
    for (int i = 0; i < items.size(); i++) {
        items[i].Expand();
    }
```

```
    ...
} else {
    response.Render(items);
    ...
}
```

On the other hand, here's a situation where the negative case *is* the simpler and more interesting/dangerous one, so we deal with it first:

```
if not file:
    # Log the error ...
else:
    # ...
```

Again, depending on the details, this may be a judgment call.

To summarize, our advice is simply to pay attention to these factors and watch out for cases where your if/else is in an awkward order.

The ?: Conditional Expression (a.k.a. "Ternary Operator")

In C-like languages, you can write a conditional expression as cond ? a : b, which is essentially a compact way to write if (cond) { a } else { b }.

Its effect on readability is controversial. Proponents think it's a nice way to write something in one line that would otherwise require multiple lines. Opponents argue that it can be confusing to read and difficult to step through in a debugger.

Here's a case where the ternary operator is readable and compact:

```
time_str += (hour >= 12) ? "pm" : "am";
```

Avoiding the ternary operator, you might write:

```
if (hour >= 12) {
    time_str += "pm";
} else {
    time_str += "am";
}
```

which is a bit drawn out and redundant. In this case, a conditional expression seems reasonable.

However, these expressions can quickly become difficult to read:

```
return exponent >= 0 ? mantissa * (1 << exponent) : mantissa / (1 << -exponent);
```

Here, the ternary operator is no longer just choosing between two simple values. The motivation for writing code like this is usually to "squeeze everything on one line."

> ## KEY IDEA
> **Instead of minimizing the number of lines, a better metric is to minimize the time needed for someone to understand it.**

Spelling out the logic with an if/else statement makes the code more natural:

```
if (exponent >= 0) {
    return mantissa * (1 << exponent);
} else {
    return mantissa / (1 << -exponent);
}
```

ADVICE

By default, use an if/else. The ternary ?: should be used only for the simplest cases.

Avoid do/while Loops

Many respected programming languages, as well as Perl, have a do { expression } while (condition) loop. The expression is executed at least once. Here's an example:

```
// Search through the list, starting at 'node', for the given 'name'.
// Don't consider more than 'max_length' nodes.
public boolean ListHasNode(Node node, String name, int max_length) {
    do {
        if (node.name().equals(name))
            return true;
        node = node.next();
    } while (node != null && --max_length > 0);

    return false;
}
```

What's weird about a do/while loop is that a block of code may or may not be reexecuted based on a condition *underneath* it. Typically, logical conditions are *above* the code they guard—this is the way it works with if, while, and for statements. Because you typically read code from top to bottom, this makes do/while a bit unnatural. Many readers end up reading the code twice.

while loops are easier to read because you know the condition for all iterations before you read the block of code inside. But it would be silly to duplicate code just to remove a do/while:

```
// Imitating a do/while - DON'T DO THIS!
body

while (condition) {
    body (again)
}
```

Fortunately, we've found that in practice most do/while loops could have been written as while loops to begin with:

```
public boolean ListHasNode(Node node, String name, int max_length) {
    while (node != null && max_length-- > 0) {
        if (node.name().equals(name)) return true;
        node = node.next();
    }
    return false;
}
```

This version also has the benefit that it still works if max_length is 0 or if node is null.

Another reason to avoid do/while is that the continue statement can be confusing inside it. For instance, what does this code do?

```
do {
    continue;
} while (false);
```

Does it loop forever or just once? Most programmers have to stop and think about it. (It should loop just once.)

Overall, Bjarne Stroustrup, the creator of C++, says it best (in *The C++ Programming Language*):

> In my experience, the do-statement is a source of errors and confusion. … I prefer the condition "up front where I can see it." Consequently, I tend to avoid do-statements.

Returning Early from a Function

Some coders believe that functions should never have multiple return statements. This is nonsense. Returning early from a function is perfectly fine—and often desirable. For example:

```
public boolean Contains(String str, String substr) {
    if (str == null || substr == null) return false;
    if (substr.equals("")) return true;
```

```
    ...
}
```

Implementing this function without these "guard clauses" would be very unnatural.

One of the motivations for wanting a single exit point is so that all the cleanup code at the bottom of the function is guaranteed to be called. But modern languages offer more sophisticated ways to achieve this guarantee:

Language	Structured idiom for cleanup code
C++	destructors
Java, Python	try finally
Python	with
C#	using

In pure C, there is no mechanism to trigger specific code when a function exits. So if there's a large function with a lot of cleanup code, returning early may be difficult to do correctly. In this case, other options include refactoring the function or even judicious use of goto cleanup;.

The Infamous goto

In languages other than C, there is little need for goto because there are so many better ways to get the job done. gotos are also notorious for getting out of hand quickly and making code difficult to follow.

But you can still see goto used in various C projects—most notably the Linux kernel. Before you dismiss all use of goto as blasphemy, it's useful to dissect why some uses of goto are better than others.

The simplest, most innocent use of goto is with a single exit at the bottom of a function:

```
    if (p == NULL) goto exit;

    ...

exit:
    fclose(file1);
    fclose(file2);
    ...

    return;
```

If this were the only form of goto allowed, goto wouldn't be much of a problem.

The problems can come when there are *multiple* goto targets, especially when their paths cross. In particular, gotos that go *upward* can make for real spaghetti code, and they can surely be replaced with structured loops. Most of the time, goto should be avoided.

Minimize Nesting

Deeply nested code is hard to understand. Each level of nesting pushes an extra condition onto the reader's "mental stack." When the reader sees a closing brace (}) it can be hard to "pop" the stack and remember what condition is underneath.

Here is a relatively simple example of this—see if you notice yourself looking back up to double-check which block conditions you're in:

```
if (user_result == SUCCESS) {
    if (permission_result != SUCCESS) {
        reply.WriteErrors("error reading permissions");
        reply.Done();
        return;
    }
    reply.WriteErrors("");
} else {
    reply.WriteErrors(user_result);

}
reply.Done();
```

When you see that first closing brace, you have to think to yourself, *Oh,* permission_result != SUCCESS *has just ended, so now* permission_result == SUCCESS, *and this is still inside the block where* user_result == SUCCESS.

Overall, you have to keep the values of user_result and permission_result in your head at all times. And as each if { } block closes, you have to toggle the corresponding value in your mind.

This particular code is even worse because it keeps alternating between the SUCCESS and non-SUCCESS situations.

How Nesting Accumulates

Before we try to fix the previous example code, let's talk about how it ended up the way it did. Originally, the code was simple:

```
if (user_result == SUCCESS) {
    reply.WriteErrors("");
} else {
    reply.WriteErrors(user_result);
}
reply.Done();
```

This code is perfectly understandable—it figures out what error string to write, and then it's done with the reply.

But then the programmer added a second operation:

```
if (user_result == SUCCESS) {
    if (permission_result != SUCCESS) {
        reply.WriteErrors("error reading permissions");
```

```
        reply.Done();
        return;
    }
    reply.WriteErrors("");

...
```

This change makes sense—the programmer had a new chunk of code to insert, and she found the easiest place to insert it. This new code was fresh and mentally "bolded" in her mind. And the "diff" of this change is very clean—it looks like a simple change.

But when someone else comes across the code later, all that context is gone. This is the way it was for you when you first read the code at the beginning of this section—you had to take it in all at once.

KEY IDEA

Look at your code from a fresh perspective when you're making changes. Step back and look at it as a whole.

Removing Nesting by Returning Early

Okay, so let's improve the code. Nesting like this can be removed by handling the "failure cases" as soon as possible and returning early from the function:

```
if (user_result != SUCCESS) {
    reply.WriteErrors(user_result);
    reply.Done();
    return;
}

if (permission_result != SUCCESS) {
    reply.WriteErrors(permission_result);
    reply.Done();
    return;
}

reply.WriteErrors("");
reply.Done();
```

This code only has one level of nesting, instead of two. But more importantly, the reader never has to "pop" anything from his mental stack—every if block ends in a return.

Removing Nesting Inside Loops

The technique of returning early isn't always applicable. For example, here's a case of code nested in a loop:

```
for (int i = 0; i < results.size(); i++) {
    if (results[i] != NULL) {
        non_null_count++;
```

```
        if (results[i]->name != "") {
            cout << "Considering candidate..." << endl;

            ...
        }
    }
}
```

Inside a loop, the analogous technique to returning early is to continue:

```
for (int i = 0; i < results.size(); i++) {
    if (results[i] == NULL) continue;
    non_null_count++;

    if (results[i]->name == "") continue;
    cout << "Considering candidate..." << endl;

    ...
}
```

In the same way that an if (...) return; acts as a guard clause for a function, these if (...) continue; statements act as guard clauses for the loop.

In general, the continue statement can be confusing, because it bounces the reader around, like a goto inside the loop. But in this case, each iteration of the loop is independent (the loop is a "for each"), so the reader can easily see that continue just means "skip over this item."

Can You Follow the Flow of Execution?

THREE-CARD MONTE

This chapter has been about low-level control flow: how to make loops, conditionals, and other jumps easy to read. But you should also think about the "flow" of your program at a high level. Ideally, it would be easy to follow the entire execution path of your program—you'd start at main() and mentally step through the code, as one function calls another, until the program exits.

In practice, however, programming languages and libraries have constructs that let code execute "behind the scenes" or make it difficult to follow. Here are some examples:

Programming construct	How high-level program flow gets obscured
threading	It's unclear what code is executed when.
signal/interrupt handlers	Certain code might be executed at any time.
exceptions	Execution can bubble up through multiple function calls.
function pointers & anonymous functions	It's hard to know exactly what code is going to run because that isn't known at compile time.
virtual methods	object.virtualMethod() might invoke code of an unknown subclass.

Some of these constructs are very useful, and they can even make your code more readable and less redundant. But as programmers, sometimes we get carried away and use them excessively without realizing how difficult it will be for readers to understand the code later. Also, these constructs make bugs much harder to track down.

The key is to not let too large a percentage of your code use these constructs. If you abuse these features, it can make tracing through your code like a game of Three-Card Monte (as in the cartoon).

Summary

There are a number of things you can do to make your code's control flow easier to read.

When writing a comparison (while (bytes_expected > bytes_received)), it's better to put the changing value on the left and the more stable value on the right (while (bytes_received < bytes_expected)).

You can also reorder the blocks of an if/else statement. Generally, try to handle the positive/easier/interesting case first. Sometimes these criteria conflict, but when they don't, it's a good rule of thumb to follow.

Certain programming constructs, like the ternary operator (: ?), the do/while loop, and goto often result in unreadable code. It's usually best not to use them, as clearer alternatives almost always exist.

Nested code blocks require more concentration to follow along. Each new nesting requires more context to be "pushed onto the stack" of the reader. Instead, opt for more "linear" code to avoid deep nesting.

Returning early can remove nesting and clean up code in general. "Guard statements" (handling simple cases at the top of the function) are especially useful.

## CHAPTER EIGHT

Breaking Down Giant Expressions

The giant squid is an amazing and intelligent animal, but its near-perfect body design has one fatal flaw: it has a donut-shaped brain that wraps around its esophagus. So if it swallows too much food at once, it gets brain damage.

What does this have to do with code? Well, code that comes in "chunks" that are too big can have the same kind of effect. Recent research suggests that most of us can only think about three or four "things" at a time.[*] Simply put, the larger an expression of code is, the harder it will be to understand.

> **KEY IDEA**
> **Break down your giant expressions into more digestible pieces.**

In this chapter, we'll go through various ways you can manipulate and break down your code so that it's easier to swallow.

Explaining Variables

The simplest way to break down an expression is to introduce an extra variable that captures a smaller subexpression. This extra variable is sometimes called an "explaining variable" because it helps explain what the subexpression means.

Here is an example:

```
if line.split(':')[0].strip() == "root":
    ...
```

Here is the same code, now with an explaining variable:

```
username = line.split(':')[0].strip()
if username == "root":
    ...
```

Summary Variables

Even if an expression doesn't *need* explaining (because you can figure out what it means), it can still be useful to capture that expression in a new variable. We call this a *summary variable* if its purpose is simply to replace a larger chunk of code with a smaller name that can be managed and thought about more easily.

For example, consider the expressions in this code:

```
if (request.user.id == document.owner_id) {
    // user can edit this document...
}
```

---

[*] Cowan, N. (2001). The magical number 4 in short-term memory: A reconsideration of mental storage capacity. *Behavioral and Brain Sciences*, 24, 97–185.

```
...

if (request.user.id != document.owner_id) {
    // document is read-only...
}
```

The expression request.user.id == document.owner_id may not seem that big, but it has five variables, so it takes a little extra time to think about.

The main concept in this code is, "Does the user own the document?" That concept can be stated more clearly by adding a summary variable:

```
final boolean user_owns_document = (request.user.id == document.owner_id);

if (user_owns_document) {
    // user can edit this document...
}

...

if (!user_owns_document) {
    // document is read-only...
}
```

It may not seem like much, but the statement if (user_owns_document) is a little easier to think about. Also, having user_owns_document defined at the top tells the reader upfront that "this is a concept we'll be referring to throughout this function."

Using De Morgan's Laws

If you ever took a course in circuits or logic, you might remember De Morgan's laws. They are two ways to rewrite a boolean expression into an equivalent one:

```
1)  not (a or b or c)    ⇔   (not a) and (not b) and (not c)
2)  not (a and b and c)  ⇔   (not a) or (not b) or (not c)
```

If you have trouble remembering these laws, a simple summary is "Distribute the not and switch and/or." (Or going the other way, you "factor out the not.")

You can sometimes use these laws to make a boolean expression more readable. For instance, if your code is:

```
if (!(file_exists && !is_protected)) Error("Sorry, could not read file.");
```

It can be rewritten to:

```
if (!file_exists || is_protected) Error("Sorry, could not read file.");
```

Abusing Short-Circuit Logic

In most programming languages, boolean operators perform short-circuit evaluation. For example, the statement if (a || b) won't evaluate b if a is true. This behavior is very handy but can sometimes be abused to accomplish complex logic.

Here is an example of a statement once written by one of the authors:

```
assert((!(bucket = FindBucket(key))) || !bucket->IsOccupied());
```

In English, what this code is saying is, "Get the bucket for this key. If the bucket is not null, then make sure it isn't occupied."

Even though it's only one line of code, it really makes most programmers stop and think. Now compare it to this code:

```
bucket = FindBucket(key);
if (bucket != NULL) assert(!bucket->IsOccupied());
```

It does exactly the same thing, and even though it's two lines of code, it's much easier to understand.

So why was the code written as a single giant expression in the first place? At the time, it felt very clever. There's a certain pleasure in paring logic down to a concise nugget of code. That's understandable—it's like solving a miniature puzzle, and we all like to have fun at work. The problem is that the code was a mental speed bump for anyone reading through the code.

> **KEY IDEA**
> Beware of "clever" nuggets of code—they're often confusing when others read the code later.

Does this mean you should avoid making use of short-circuit behavior? No. There are plenty of cases where it can be used cleanly, for instance:

```
if (object && object->method()) ...
```

There is also a newer idiom worth mentioning: in languages like Python, JavaScript, and Ruby, the "or" operator returns one of its arguments (it doesn't convert to a boolean), so code like:

```
x = a || b || c
```

can be used to pick out the first "truthy" value from a, b, or c.

Example: Wrestling with Complicated Logic

Suppose you're implementing the following Range class:

```
struct Range {
    int begin;
    int end;
```

```
    // For example, [0,5) overlaps with [3,8)
    bool OverlapsWith(Range other);
};
```

The following figure shows some example ranges:

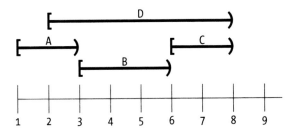

Note that end is noninclusive. So A, B, and C don't overlap with each other, but D overlaps with all of them.

Here is one attempt at implementing OverlapsWith()—it checks if either endpoint of its range falls inside the other's range:

```
bool Range::OverlapsWith(Range other) {
    // Check if 'begin' or 'end' falls inside 'other'.
    return (begin >= other.begin && begin <= other.end) ||
           (end >= other.begin && end <= other.end);
}
```

Even though the code is only two lines long, there's a lot going on. The following figure shows all the logic involved.

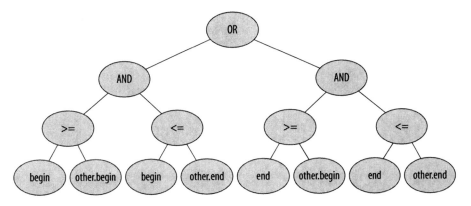

There are so many cases and conditions to think about that it's easy for a bug to slip by.

Speaking of which, there *is* a bug. The previous code will claim that the Range [0,2) overlaps with [2,4) when in fact it doesn't.

The problem is that you have to be careful when comparing begin/end values using <= or just <. Here's a fix to this problem:

```
return (begin >= other.begin && begin < other.end) ||
       (end > other.begin && end <= other.end);
```

Now it's correct, right? Actually, there's *another* bug. This code has ignored the case when begin/end completely surround other.

Here's a fix that handles this case, too:

```
return (begin >= other.begin && begin < other.end) ||
       (end > other.begin && end <= other.end) ||
       (begin <= other.begin && end >= other.end);
```

Yikes—this code has become way too complicated. You can't expect anyone to read this code and confidently know that it's correct. So what do we do? How can we break down this giant expression?

Finding a More Elegant Approach

This is one of those times when you should stop and consider a different approach altogether. What started as a simple problem (checking whether two ranges overlap) turned into a surprisingly convoluted piece of logic. This is often a sign that **there must be an easier way.**

But finding a more elegant solution takes creativity. How do you go about it? One technique is to see if you can solve the problem the "opposite" way. Depending on the situation you're in, this could mean iterating through arrays in reverse or filling in some data structure backward rather than forward.

Here, the opposite of OverlapsWith() is "doesn't overlap." Determining if two ranges *don't* overlap turns out to be a much simpler problem, because there are only two possibilities:

1. The other range ends before this one begins.
2. The other range begins after this one ends.

We can turn this into code quite easily:

```
bool Range::OverlapsWith(Range other) {
    if (other.end <= begin) return false;  // They end before we begin
    if (other.begin >= end) return false;  // They begin after we end

    return true;  // Only possibility left: they overlap
}
```

Each line of code here is much simpler—it involves only a single comparison. That leaves the reader with enough brainpower to focus on whether <= is correct.

Breaking Down Giant Statements

This chapter is about breaking down individual expressions, but the same techniques apply to breaking down larger statements as well. For example, the following JavaScript code has a lot to take in at once:

```javascript
var update_highlight = function (message_num) {
    if ($("#vote_value" + message_num).html() === "Up") {
        $("#thumbs_up" + message_num).addClass("highlighted");
        $("#thumbs_down" + message_num).removeClass("highlighted");
    } else if ($("#vote_value" + message_num).html() === "Down") {
        $("#thumbs_up" + message_num).removeClass("highlighted");
        $("#thumbs_down" + message_num).addClass("highlighted");
    } else {
        $("#thumbs_up" + message_num).removeClass("highlighted");
        $("#thumbs_down" + message_num).removeClass("highlighted");
    }
};
```

The individual expressions in this code aren't that big, but when placed all together, it forms one giant statement that hits you all at once.

Fortunately, a lot of the expressions are the same, which means we can extract them out as summary variables at the top of the function (this is also an instance of the DRY—Don't Repeat Yourself—principle):

```javascript
var update_highlight = function (message_num) {
    var thumbs_up = $("#thumbs_up" + message_num);
    var thumbs_down = $("#thumbs_down" + message_num);
    var vote_value = $("#vote_value" + message_num).html();
    var hi = "highlighted";

    if (vote_value === "Up") {
        thumbs_up.addClass(hi);
        thumbs_down.removeClass(hi);
    } else if (vote_value === "Down") {
        thumbs_up.removeClass(hi);
        thumbs_down.addClass(hi);
    } else {
        thumbs_up.removeClass(hi);
        thumbs_down.removeClass(hi);
    }
};
```

The creation of `var hi = "highlighted"` isn't strictly needed, but as there were *six* copies of it, there were compelling benefits:

- It helps avoid typing mistakes. (In fact, did you notice that in the first example, the string was misspelled as "highighted" in the fifth case?)

- It shrinks the line width even more, making the code easier to scan through.

- If the class name needed to change, there's just one place to change it.

Another Creative Way to Simplify Expressions

Here's another example with a lot going on in each expression, this time in C++:

```cpp
void AddStats(const Stats& add_from, Stats* add_to) {
    add_to->set_total_memory(add_from.total_memory() + add_to->total_memory());
    add_to->set_free_memory(add_from.free_memory() + add_to->free_memory());
    add_to->set_swap_memory(add_from.swap_memory() + add_to->swap_memory());
    add_to->set_status_string(add_from.status_string() + add_to->status_string());
    add_to->set_num_processes(add_from.num_processes() + add_to->num_processes());
    ...
}
```

Once again, your eyes are faced with code that's long and similar, but not exactly the same. After ten seconds of careful scrutiny, you might realize that each line is doing the same thing, just to a different field each time:

```cpp
add_to->set_XXX(add_from.XXX() + add_to->XXX());
```

In C++, we can define a macro to implement this:

```cpp
void AddStats(const Stats& add_from, Stats* add_to) {
    #define ADD_FIELD(field) add_to->set_##field(add_from.field() + add_to->field())

    ADD_FIELD(total_memory);
    ADD_FIELD(free_memory);
    ADD_FIELD(swap_memory);
    ADD_FIELD(status_string);
    ADD_FIELD(num_processes);
    ...
    #undef ADD_FIELD
}
```

Now that we've stripped away all the clutter, you can look at the code and immediately understand the essence of what's happening. It's very clear that each line is doing the same thing.

Note that we're not advocating using macros very often—in fact, we usually avoid them because they can make code confusing and introduce subtle bugs. But sometimes, as in this case, they're simple and can provide a clear benefit to readability.

Summary

Giant expressions are hard to think about. This chapter showed a number of ways to break them down so the reader can digest them piece by piece.

One simple technique is to introduce "explaining variables" that capture the value of some large subexpression. This approach has three benefits:

- It breaks down a giant expression into pieces.
- It documents the code by describing the subexpression with a succinct name.
- It helps the reader identify the main "concepts" in the code.

Another technique is to manipulate your logic using De Morgan's laws—this technique can sometimes rewrite a boolean expression in a cleaner way (e.g., if (!(a && !b)) turns into if (!a || b)).

We showed an example where a complex logical condition was broken down into tiny statements like "if (a < b) ...". In fact, *all* of the improved-code examples in this chapter had if statements with no more than *two* values inside them. This setup is ideal. It may not always seem possible to do this—sometimes it requires "negating" the problem or considering the opposite of your goal.

Finally, even though this chapter is about breaking down individual expressions, these same techniques often apply to larger blocks of code, too. So be aggressive in breaking down complex logic wherever you see it.

## CHAPTER NINE

Variables and Readability

THE RINGMASTER'S HOUSE

In this chapter, you'll see how sloppy use of *variables* makes a program harder to understand. Specifically, there are three problems to contend with:

1. The more variables there are, the harder it is to keep track of them all.
2. The bigger a variable's scope, the longer you have to keep track of it.
3. The more often a variable changes, the harder it is to keep track of its current value.

The next three sections discuss how to deal with these issues.

Eliminating Variables

In Chapter 8, *Breaking Down Giant Expressions*, we showed how introducing "explaining" or "summary" variables can make code more readable. These variables were helpful because they broke down giant expressions and acted as a form of documentation.

In this section, we're interested in eliminating variables that *don't* improve readability. When a variable like this is removed, the new code is more concise and just as easy to understand.

In the following section are a few examples of how these unnecessary variables show up.

Useless Temporary Variables

In the following snippet of Python code, consider the now variable:

```
now = datetime.datetime.now()
root_message.last_view_time = now
```

Is now a variable worth keeping? No, and here are the reasons:

- It isn't breaking down a complex expression.
- It doesn't add clarification—the expression datetime.datetime.now() is clear enough.
- It's used only once, so it doesn't compress any redundant code.

Without now, the code is just as easy to understand:

```
root_message.last_view_time = datetime.datetime.now()
```

Variables like now are usually "leftovers" that remain after code has been edited. The variable now might have been used in multiple places originally. Or maybe the coder anticipated using now multiple times, but never actually needed it.

Eliminating Intermediate Results

Here's an example of a JavaScript function that removes a value from an array:

```javascript
var remove_one = function (array, value_to_remove) {
    var index_to_remove = null;
    for (var i = 0; i < array.length; i += 1) {
        if (array[i] === value_to_remove) {
            index_to_remove = i;
            break;
        }
    }
    if (index_to_remove !== null) {
        array.splice(index_to_remove, 1);
    }
};
```

The variable index_to_remove is just used to hold an *intermediate result*. Variables like this can sometimes be eliminated by handling the result as soon as you get it:

```javascript
var remove_one = function (array, value_to_remove) {
    for (var i = 0; i < array.length; i += 1) {
        if (array[i] === value_to_remove) {
            array.splice(i, 1);
            return;
        }
    }
};
```

By allowing the code to return early, we got rid of index_to_remove altogether and simplified the code quite a bit.

In general, it's a good strategy to **complete the task as quickly as possible**.

Eliminating Control Flow Variables

Sometimes you'll see this pattern of code in loops:

```
boolean done = false;

while (/* condition */ && !done) {
    ...

    if (...) {
        done = true;
        continue;
    }
}
```

The variable done might even be set to true in multiple places throughout the loop.

Code like this is often trying to satisfy some unspoken rule that you shouldn't break out of the middle of a loop. There is no such rule!

Variables like done are what we call "control flow variables." Their sole purpose is to steer the program's execution—they don't contain any real program data. In our experience, control flow variables can often be eliminated by making better use of structured programming:

```
while (/* condition */) {
    ...
    if (...) {
        break;
    }
}
```

This case was pretty easy to fix, but what if there are *multiple* nested loops for which a simple break wouldn't suffice? In more complicated cases like that, the solution often involves moving code into a new function (either the code inside the loop, or the entire loop itself).

DO YOU WANT YOUR COWORKERS TO FEEL LIKE THEY'RE IN AN INTERVIEW ALL THE TIME?

Microsoft's Eric Brechner has talked about how a great interview question should involve at least three variables.[*] It's probably because dealing with three variables at the same time forces you to think hard! This makes sense for an interview, where you're trying to push a candidate to the limit. But do you want your coworkers to feel like they're in an interview while they're reading your code?

---

* Eric Brechner's *I. M. Wright's "Hard Code"* (Microsoft Press, 2007), p. 166.

Shrink the Scope of Your Variables

We've all heard the advice to "avoid global variables." This is good advice, because it's hard to keep track of where and how all those global variables are being used. And by "polluting the namespace" (putting a bunch of names there that might conflict with your local variables), code might accidentally modify a global variable when it intended to use a local variable, or vice versa.

In fact, it's a good idea to "shrink the scope" of *all* your variables, not just the global ones.

KEY IDEA
Make your variable visible by as few lines of code as possible.

Many programming languages offer multiple scope/access levels, including module, class, function, and block scope. Using more restricted access is generally better because it means the variable can be "seen" by fewer lines of code.

Why do this? Because it effectively reduces the number of variables the reader has to think about at the same time. If you were to shrink the scope of all your variables by a factor of two, then on average there would be half as many variables in scope at any one time.

For example, suppose you have a very large class, with a member variable that's used by only two methods, in the following way:

```
class LargeClass {
    string str_;

    void Method1() {
        str_ = ...;
        Method2();
    }

    void Method2() {
        // Uses str_
    }

    // Lots of other methods that don't use str_ ...
};
```

In some sense, a class member variable is like a "mini-global" inside the realm of the class. For large classes especially, it's hard to keep track of all the member variables and which methods modify each one. The fewer mini-globals, the better.

For this case, it may make sense to "demote" str_ to be a local variable:

```
class LargeClass {
    void Method1() {
        string str = ...;
        Method2(str);
    }
```

```
    void Method2(string str) {
        // Uses str
    }

    // Now other methods can't see str.
};
```

Another way to restrict access to class members is to **make as many methods static as possible**. Static methods are a great way to let the reader know "these lines of code are isolated from those variables."

Or another approach is to **break the large class into smaller classes**. This approach is helpful only if the smaller classes are in fact isolated from each other. If you were to create two classes that access each other's members, you haven't really accomplished anything.

The same goes for breaking up large files into smaller files or large functions into smaller functions. A big motivation for doing so is to isolate data (i.e., variables).

But different languages have different rules for what exactly constitutes a scope. We'd like to point out just a few of the more interesting rules involving the scope of variables.

if Statement Scope in C++

Suppose you have the following C++ code:

```
PaymentInfo* info = database.ReadPaymentInfo();
if (info) {
    cout << "User paid: " << info->amount() << endl;
}

// Many more lines of code below ...
```

The variable info will remain in scope for the rest of the function, so the person reading this code might keep info in mind, wondering if/how it will be used again.

But in this case, info is only used inside the if statement. In C++, we can actually define info in the conditional expression:

```
if (PaymentInfo* info = database.ReadPaymentInfo()) {
    cout << "User paid: " << info->amount() << endl;
}
```

Now the reader can easily forget about info after it goes out of scope.

Creating "Private" Variables in JavaScript

Suppose you have a persistent variable that's used by only one function:

```
submitted = false;  // Note: global variable

var submit_form = function (form_name) {
    if (submitted) {
        return;  // don't double-submit the form
    }
    ...
    submitted = true;
};
```

Global variables like submitted can cause the person reading this code a lot of angst. It seems like submit_form() is the only function that uses submitted, but you can't know for sure. In fact, another JavaScript file might be using a global variable named submitted too, for a different purpose!

You can prevent this issue by wrapping submitted inside a *closure*:

```
var submit_form = (function () {
    var submitted = false;  // Note: can only be accessed by the function below

    return function (form_name) {
        if (submitted) {
            return;  // don't double-submit the form
        }
        ...
        submitted = true;
    };
}());
```

Note the parentheses on the last line—the anonymous outer function is immediately executed, returning the inner function.

If you haven't seen this technique before, it may look strange at first. It has the effect of making a "private" scope that only the inner function can access. Now the reader doesn't have to wonder *Where else does* submitted *get used?* or worry about conflicting with other globals of the same name. (See *JavaScript: The Good Parts* by Douglas Crockford [O'Reilly, 2008] for more techniques like this.)

JavaScript Global Scope

In JavaScript, if you omit the keyword var from a variable definition (e.g., x = 1 instead of var x = 1), the variable is put into the global scope, where *every* JavaScript file and <script> block can access it. Here is an example:

```
<script>
    var f = function () {
        // DANGER: 'i' is not declared with 'var'!
        for (i = 0; i < 10; i += 1) ...
    };

    f();
</script>
```

This code inadvertently puts i into the global scope, so a later block can still see it:

```
<script>
    alert(i);  // Alerts '10'.  'i' is a global variable!
</script>
```

Many programmers aren't aware of this scoping rule, and this surprising behavior can cause strange bugs. A common manifestation of this bug is when two functions both create a local variable with the same name, but forget to use var. These functions will unknowingly "cross-talk" and the poor programmer might conclude that his computer is possessed or that his RAM has gone bad.

The common "best practice" for JavaScript is to **always define variables using the** var **keyword** (e.g., var x = 1). This practice limits the scope of the variable to the (innermost) function where it's defined.

No Nested Scope in Python and JavaScript

Languages like C++ and Java have *block scope*, where variables defined inside an if, for, try, or similar structure are confined to the nested scope of that block:

```
if (...) {
    int x = 1;
}
x++;  // Compile-error! 'x' is undefined.
```

But in Python and JavaScript, variables defined in a block "spill out" to the whole function. For example, notice the use of example_value in this perfectly valid Python code:

```
# No use of example_value up to this point.
if request:
    for value in request.values:
        if value > 0:
            example_value = value
            break

for logger in debug.loggers:
    logger.log("Example:", example_value)
```

This scoping rule is surprising to many programmers, and code like this is harder to read. In other languages, it would be easier to find where example_value was first defined—you would look along the "left-hand edge" of the function you're inside.

The previous example is also buggy: if example_value is not set in the first part of the code, the second part will raise an exception: "NameError: 'example_value' is not defined". We can fix this, and make the code more readable, by defining example_value at the "closest common ancestor" (in terms of nesting) to where it's used:

```
example_value = None

if request:
    for value in request.values:
        if value > 0:
            example_value = value
            break

if example_value:
    for logger in debug.loggers:
        logger.log("Example:", example_value)
```

However, this is a case where example_value can be eliminated altogether. example_value is just holding an intermediate result, and as we saw in "Eliminating Intermediate Results" on page 95, variables like these can often be eliminated by "completing the task as soon as possible." In this case, that means logging the example value as soon as we find it.

Here's what the new code looks like:

```
def LogExample(value):
    for logger in debug.loggers:
        logger.log("Example:", value)

if request:
    for value in request.values:
        if value > 0:
            LogExample(value)  # deal with 'value' immediately
            break
```

Moving Definitions Down

The original C programming language required all variable definitions to be at the top of the function or block. This requirement was unfortunate, because for long functions with many variables, it forced the reader to think about all those variables right away, even if they weren't used until much later. (C99 and C++ removed this requirement.)

In the following example, all the variables are innocently defined at the top of the function:

```
def ViewFilteredReplies(original_id):
    filtered_replies = []
    root_message = Messages.objects.get(original_id)
    all_replies = Messages.objects.select(root_id=original_id)
```

```
        root_message.view_count += 1
        root_message.last_view_time = datetime.datetime.now()
        root_message.save()

        for reply in all_replies:
            if reply.spam_votes <= MAX_SPAM_VOTES:
                filtered_replies.append(reply)

        return filtered_replies
```

The problem with this example code is that it forces the reader to think about three variables at once, and switch gears between them.

Because the reader doesn't need to know about all of them until later, it's easy to just move each definition right before its first use:

```
    def ViewFilteredReplies(original_id):
        root_message = Messages.objects.get(original_id)
        root_message.view_count += 1
        root_message.last_view_time = datetime.datetime.now()
        root_message.save()

        all_replies = Messages.objects.select(root_id=original_id)
        filtered_replies = []
        for reply in all_replies:
            if reply.spam_votes <= MAX_SPAM_VOTES:
                filtered_replies.append(reply)

        return filtered_replies
```

You might be wondering whether all_replies is a necessary variable, or if it could be eliminated by doing:

```
        for reply in Messages.objects.select(root_id=original_id):
            ...
```

In this case, all_replies is a pretty good explaining variable, so we decided to keep it.

Prefer Write-Once Variables

So far in this chapter, we've discussed how it's harder to understand programs with lots of variables "in play." Well, it's even harder to think about variables that are constantly changing. Keeping track of their values adds an extra degree of difficulty.

To combat this problem, we have a suggestion that may sound a little strange: **prefer write-once variables**.

Variables that are a "permanent fixture" are easier to think about. Certainly, constants like:

```
static const int NUM_THREADS = 10;
```

don't require much thought on the reader's part. And for the same reason, use of `const` in C++ (and `final` in Java) is highly encouraged.

In fact, in many languages (including Python and Java), some built-in types like `string` are *immutable*. As James Gosling (Java's creator) said, "[Immutables] tend to more often be trouble free."

But even if you can't make your variable write-once, it still helps if the variable changes in fewer places.

> **KEY IDEA**
>
> **The more places a variable is manipulated, the harder it is to reason about its current value.**

So how do you do it? How can you change a variable to be write-once? Well, a lot of times it requires restructuring the code a bit, as you'll see in the next example.

A Final Example

For the final example of the chapter, we'd like to show an example demonstrating many of the principles we've discussed so far.

Suppose you have a web page with a number of input text fields, arranged like this:

```
<input type="text" id="input1" value="Dustin">
<input type="text" id="input2" value="Trevor">
<input type="text" id="input3" value="">
<input type="text" id="input4" value="Melissa">
...
```

As you can see, the ids start with `input1` and increment from there.

Your job is to write a function named `setFirstEmptyInput()` that takes a string and puts it in the first empty `<input>` on the page (in the example shown, `"input3"`). The function should return the DOM element that was updated (or `null` if there were no empty inputs left). Here is some code to do this that *doesn't* apply the principles in this chapter:

```
var setFirstEmptyInput = function (new_value) {
    var found = false;
    var i = 1;
    var elem = document.getElementById('input' + i);
    while (elem !== null) {
        if (elem.value === '') {
            found = true;
            break;
        }
        i++;
        elem = document.getElementById('input' + i);
    }
```

```
        if (found) elem.value = new_value;
        return elem;
    };
```

This code gets the job done, but it's not pretty. What's wrong with it, and how do we improve it?

There are a lot of ways to think about improving this code, but we're going to consider it from the perspective of the variables it uses:

- `var found`
- `var i`
- `var elem`

All three of these variables exist for the entire function and are written to multiple times. Let's try to improve the use of each of them.

As we discussed earlier in the chapter, intermediate variables like `found` can often be eliminated by returning early. Here's that improvement:

```
    var setFirstEmptyInput = function (new_value) {
        var i = 1;
        var elem = document.getElementById('input' + i);
        while (elem !== null) {
            if (elem.value === '') {
                elem.value = new_value;
                return elem;
            }
            i++;
            elem = document.getElementById('input' + i);
        }
        return null;
    };
```

Next, take a look at elem. It's used multiple times throughout the code in a very "loopy" way where it's hard to keep track of its value. The code makes it seem as if elem is the value we're iterating through, when really we're just incrementing through i. So let's restructure the while loop into a for loop over i:

```
    var setFirstEmptyInput = function (new_value) {
        for (var i = 1; true; i++) {
            var elem = document.getElementById('input' + i);
            if (elem === null)
                return null;  // Search Failed. No empty input found.

            if (elem.value === '') {
                elem.value = new_value;
                return elem;
            }
        }
    };
```

In particular, notice how `elem` acts as a write-once variable whose lifespan is contained inside the loop. The use of `true` as a `for` loop condition is unusual, but in exchange, we are able to see the definition and modifications of `i` in a single line. (A traditional `while (true)` would also be reasonable.)

Summary

This chapter is about how the variables in a program can quickly accumulate and become too much to keep track of. You can make your code easier to read by having fewer variables and making them as "lightweight" as possible. Specifically:

- **Eliminate variables** that just get in the way. In particular, we showed a few examples of how to eliminate "intermediate result" variables by handling the result immediately.
- **Reduce the scope of each variable** to be as small as possible. Move each variable to a place where the fewest lines of code can see it. Out of sight is out of mind.
- **Prefer write-once variables.** Variables that are set only once (or `const`, `final`, or otherwise immutable) make code easier to understand.

## PART III

Reorganizing Your Code

In Part II, we discussed how to change the "loops and logic" of your program to make your code more readable. We described several techniques that required changing the structure of your program in minor ways.

In this part, we'll discuss larger changes you can make to your code at the function level. Specifically, we'll cover three ways to reorganize your code:

- Extract "unrelated subproblems" that aren't related to the primary goal of your program.
- Rearrange your code so it's doing only one task at a time.
- Describe your code in words first, and use this description to help guide you to a cleaner solution.

Finally, we'll discuss situations where you can remove code entirely or avoid writing it in the first place—the single best way to make code easy to understand.

## CHAPTER TEN

Extracting Unrelated Subproblems

Engineering is all about breaking down big problems into smaller ones and putting the solutions for those problems back together. Applying this principle to code makes it more robust and easier to read.

The advice for this chapter is to **aggressively identify and extract unrelated subproblems.** Here's what we mean:

1. Look at a given function or block of code, and ask yourself, "What is the high-level goal of this code?"

2. For each line of code, ask, "Is it working *directly* to that goal? Or is it solving an *unrelated subproblem* needed to meet it?"

3. If enough lines are solving an unrelated subproblem, extract that code into a separate function.

Extracting code into separate functions is something you probably do every day. But for this chapter, we decided to focus on the specific case of extracting *unrelated subproblems,* where the extracted code is blissfully unaware of why it's being called.

As you'll see, it's an easy technique to apply but can improve your code substantially. Yet for some reason, many programmers don't use this technique enough. The trick is to actively look for these unrelated subproblems.

In this chapter, we will go through a variety of examples that illustrate this technique for different situations you might run into.

Introductory Example: findClosestLocation()

The high-level goal of the following JavaScript code is, *find the location that's closest to a given point* (don't get bogged down by the advanced geometry, which we've italicized):

```
// Return which element of 'array' is closest to the given latitude/longitude.
// Models the Earth as a perfect sphere.
var findClosestLocation = function (lat, lng, array) {
    var closest;
    var closest_dist = Number.MAX_VALUE;
    for (var i = 0; i < array.length; i += 1) {
        // Convert both points to radians.
        var lat_rad = radians(lat);
        var lng_rad = radians(lng);
        var lat2_rad = radians(array[i].latitude);
        var lng2_rad = radians(array[i].longitude);

        // Use the "Spherical Law of Cosines" formula.
        var dist = Math.acos(Math.sin(lat_rad) * Math.sin(lat2_rad) +
                             Math.cos(lat_rad) * Math.cos(lat2_rad) *
                             Math.cos(lng2_rad - lng_rad));

        if (dist < closest_dist) {
            closest = array[i];
```

```
                closest_dist = dist;
            }
        }
        return closest;
    };
```

Most of the code inside the loop is working on an unrelated subproblem: *Compute the spherical distance between two lat/long points.* Because there is so much of that code, it makes sense to extract it into a separate spherical_distance() function:

```
    var spherical_distance = function (lat1, lng1, lat2, lng2) {
        var lat1_rad = radians(lat1);
        var lng1_rad = radians(lng1);
        var lat2_rad = radians(lat2);
        var lng2_rad = radians(lng2);

        // Use the "Spherical Law of Cosines" formula.
        return Math.acos(Math.sin(lat1_rad) * Math.sin(lat2_rad) +
                         Math.cos(lat1_rad) * Math.cos(lat2_rad) *
                         Math.cos(lng2_rad - lng1_rad));
    };
```

Now the remaining code becomes:

```
    var findClosestLocation = function (lat, lng, array) {
        var closest;
        var closest_dist = Number.MAX_VALUE;
        for (var i = 0; i < array.length; i += 1) {
            var dist = spherical_distance(lat, lng, array[i].latitude, array[i].longitude);
            if (dist < closest_dist) {
                closest = array[i];
                closest_dist = dist;
            }
        }
        return closest;
    };
```

This code is far more readable because the reader can focus on the high-level goal without getting distracted by intense geometry equations.

As an added bonus, spherical_distance() will be easier to test in isolation. And spherical_distance() is the type of function that could be reused in the future. This is why it's an "unrelated" subproblem—it's completely self-contained and unaware of how applications are using it.

Pure Utility Code

There is a core set of basic tasks that most programs do, such as manipulating strings, using hash tables, and reading/writing files.

Often, these "basic utilities" are implemented by the built-in libraries in your programming language. For instance, if you want to read the entire contents of a file, in PHP you can call file_get_contents("filename"), or in Python, you can do open("filename").read().

But sometimes you have to fill in the gaps yourself. In C++, for instance, there is no succinct way to read an entire file. Instead, you inevitably end up writing code like this:

```
ifstream file(file_name);

// Calculate the file's size, and allocate a buffer of that size.
file.seekg(0, ios::end);
const int file_size = file.tellg();
char* file_buf = new char [file_size];

// Read the entire file into the buffer.
file.seekg(0, ios::beg);
file.read(file_buf, file_size);
file.close();

...
```

This is a classic example of an unrelated subproblem that should be extracted into a new function like ReadFileToString(). Now, the rest of your codebase can act as if C++ *did* have a ReadFileToString() function.

In general, if you find yourself thinking, "I wish our library had an XYZ() function," go ahead and write it! (Assuming it doesn't already exist.) Over time, you'll build up a nice collection of utility code that can be used across projects.

Other General-Purpose Code

When debugging JavaScript, programmers often use alert() to pop up a message box that displays some information to the programmer, the Web's version of "printf() debugging." For example, the following function call submits data to the server using Ajax and then displays the dictionary returned from the server:

```
ajax_post({
    url: 'http://example.com/submit',
    data: data,
    on_success: function (response_data) {
        var str = "{\n";
        for (var key in response_data) {
            str += "  " + key + " = " + response_data[key] + "\n";
        }
        alert(str + "}");

        // Continue handling 'response_data' ...
    }
});
```

The high-level goal of this code is, *Make an Ajax call to the server, and handle the response.* But a lot of the code is solving the unrelated subproblem, *Pretty-print a dictionary.* It's easy to extract that code into a function like format_pretty(obj):

```
var format_pretty = function (obj) {
    var str = "{\n";
    for (var key in obj) {
        str += "    " + key + " = " + obj[key] + "\n";
    }
    return str + "}";
};
```

Unexpected Benefits

There are a lot of reasons why extracting format_pretty() is a good idea. It makes the calling code simpler, and format_pretty() is a handy function to have around.

But there's another great reason that's not as obvious: **it's easier to improve** format_pretty() **when the code is by itself.** When you're working on a smaller function in isolation, it feels easier to add features, improve reliability, take care of edge cases, and so on.

Here are some cases format_pretty(obj) doesn't handle:

- It expects obj to be an object. If instead it's a plain string (or undefined), the current code will throw an exception.
- It expects each value of obj to be a simple type. If instead it contains nested objects, the current code will display them as [object Object], which isn't very pretty.

Before we separated format_pretty() into its own function, it would have felt like a lot of work to make all these improvements. (In fact, recursively printing nested objects is very difficult without a separate function.)

But now, adding this functionality is easy. Here's what the improved code looks like:

```
var format_pretty = function (obj, indent) {
    // Handle null, undefined, strings, and non-objects.
    if (obj === null) return "null";
    if (obj === undefined) return "undefined";
    if (typeof obj === "string") return '"' + obj + '"';
    if (typeof obj !== "object") return String(obj);

    if (indent === undefined) indent = "";

    // Handle (non-null) objects.
    var str = "{\n";
    for (var key in obj) {
        str += indent + "    " + key + " = ";
        str += format_pretty(obj[key], indent + "    ") + "\n";
    }
    return str + indent + "}";
};
```

This covers the shortcomings listed previously and produces output like this:

```
{
    key1 = 1
    key2 = true
    key3 = undefined
    key4 = null
    key5 = {
        key5a = {
            key5a1 = "hello world"
        }
    }
}
```

Create a Lot of General-Purpose Code

The functions ReadFileToString() and format_pretty() are great examples of unrelated subproblems. They're so basic and widely applicable that they are likely to be reused across projects. Codebases often have a special directory for code like this (e.g., util/) so that it can be easily shared.

General-purpose code is great because **it's completely decoupled from the rest of your project.** Code like this is easier to develop, easier to test, and easier to understand. If only all of your code could be like this!

Think about many of the powerful libraries and systems that you use, such as SQL databases, JavaScript libraries, and HTML templating systems. You don't have to worry about their internals—those codebases are completely isolated from your project. As a result, your project's codebase remains small.

The more of your project you can break away as isolated libraries, the better, because the rest of your code will be smaller and easier to think about.

IS THIS TOP-DOWN OR BOTTOM-UP PROGRAMMING?

Top-down programming is a style where the highest-level modules and functions are designed first and the lower-level functions are implemented as needed to support them.

Bottom-up programming tries to anticipate and solve all the subproblems first and then build the higher-level components using these pieces.

This chapter isn't advocating one method over the other. Most programming involves a combination of both. What's important is the end result: subproblems are removed and tackled separately.

Project-Specific Functionality

Ideally, the subproblems you extract would be completely project-agnostic. But even if they're not, that's okay. Breaking off subproblems still works wonders.

Here is an example from a business reviews website. This Python code creates a new Business object and sets its `name`, `url`, and `date_created`:

```python
business = Business()
business.name = request.POST["name"]

url_path_name = business.name.lower()
url_path_name = re.sub(r"['\.]", "", url_path_name)
url_path_name = re.sub(r"[^a-z0-9]+", "-", url_path_name)
url_path_name = url_path_name.strip("-")
business.url = "/biz/" + url_path_name

business.date_created = datetime.datetime.utcnow()
business.save_to_database()
```

The `url` is supposed to be a "clean" version of the `name`. For example, if the `name` is "A.C. Joe's Tire & Smog, Inc.," the `url` will be "/biz/ac-joes-tire-smog-inc".

The unrelated subproblem in this code is: *Turn a name into a valid URL.* We can extract this code quite easily. While we're at it, we can also precompile the regular expressions (and give them readable names):

```python
CHARS_TO_REMOVE = re.compile(r"['\.]+")
CHARS_TO_DASH = re.compile(r"[^a-z0-9]+")

def make_url_friendly(text):
    text = text.lower()
    text = CHARS_TO_REMOVE.sub('', text)
    text = CHARS_TO_DASH.sub('-', text)
    return text.strip("-")
```

Now the original code has a much more "regular" pattern:

```python
business = Business()
business.name = request.POST["name"]
business.url = "/biz/" + make_url_friendly(business.name)
business.date_created = datetime.datetime.utcnow()
business.save_to_database()
```

This code requires far less effort to read because you aren't distracted by the regular expressions and deep string manipulation.

Where should you put the code for `make_url_friendly()`? It seems like a fairly general function, so it might make sense to put it in a separate `util/` directory. On the other hand, those regular expressions were designed with U.S. business names in mind, so perhaps the code should stay in the same file where it's used. It actually doesn't matter that much, and you can easily move the definition later on. What's more important is that `make_url_friendly()` was extracted at all.

Simplifying an Existing Interface

Everybody loves when a library offers a clean interface—one that takes few arguments, doesn't need much setup, and generally requires little effort to use. It makes your code look elegant: simple and powerful at the same time.

But if an interface you're using isn't clean, you can still make your own "wrapper" functions that are.

For example, dealing with browser cookies in JavaScript is far from ideal. Conceptually, cookies are a set of name/value pairs. But the interface the browser provides presents a single document.cookie string whose syntax is:

```
name1=value1; name2=value2; ...
```

To find the cookie you want, you're forced to parse this giant string yourself. Here's an example of code that reads the value for the cookie named "max_results":

```
var max_results;
var cookies = document.cookie.split(';');
for (var i = 0; i < cookies.length; i++) {
    var c = cookies[i];
    c = c.replace(/^[ ]+/, '');  // remove leading spaces
    if (c.indexOf("max_results=") === 0)
        max_results = Number(c.substring(12, c.length));
}
```

Wow, that's some ugly code. Clearly, there's a get_cookie() function waiting to be made so that we can just write:

```
var max_results = Number(get_cookie("max_results"));
```

Creating or changing a cookie value is even stranger. You have to set document.cookie to a value with an exact syntax:

```
document.cookie = "max_results=50; expires=Wed, 1 Jan 2020 20:53:47 UTC; path=/";
```

That statement looks like it would overwrite all other existing cookies, but (magically) it doesn't!

A more ideal interface to setting a cookie would be something like:

```
set_cookie(name, value, days_to_expire);
```

Erasing a cookie is also unintuitive: you have to set the cookie to expire in the past. Instead, an ideal interface would be simply:

```
delete_cookie(name);
```

The lesson here is that **you should never have to settle for an interface that's less than ideal.** You can always create your own wrapper functions to hide the ugly details of an interface you're stuck with.

Reshaping an Interface to Your Needs

A lot of code in a program is there just to support other code—for example, setting up inputs to a function or postprocessing the output. This "glue" code often has nothing to do with the real logic of your program. Mundane code like this is a great candidate to be pulled out into separate functions.

For example, let's say you have a Python dictionary containing sensitive user information like { "username": "...", "password": "..." } and you need to put all that information into a URL. Because it's sensitive, you decide to encrypt the dictionary first, using a Cipher class.

But Cipher expects a string of bytes as input, not a dictionary. And Cipher returns a string of bytes, but we need something that's URL-safe. Cipher also takes a number of extra parameters and is pretty cumbersome to use.

What started as a simple task turns into a lot of glue code:

```
user_info = { "username": "...", "password": "..." }
user_str = json.dumps(user_info)
cipher = Cipher("aes_128_cbc", key=PRIVATE_KEY, init_vector=INIT_VECTOR, op=ENCODE)
encrypted_bytes = cipher.update(user_str)
encrypted_bytes += cipher.final()  # flush out the current 128 bit block
url = "http://example.com/?user_info=" + base64.urlsafe_b64encode(encrypted_bytes)
...
```

Even though the problem we're tackling is *Encrypt the user's information into a URL,* the majority of this code is just doing *Encrypt this Python object into a URL-friendly string.* It's easy to extract that subproblem:

```
def url_safe_encrypt(obj):
    obj_str = json.dumps(obj)
    cipher = Cipher("aes_128_cbc", key=PRIVATE_KEY, init_vector=INIT_VECTOR, op=ENCODE)
    encrypted_bytes = cipher.update(obj_str)
    encrypted_bytes += cipher.final()  # flush out the current 128 bit block
    return base64.urlsafe_b64encode(encrypted_bytes)
```

Then, the resulting code to execute the *real* logic of the program is simple:

```
user_info = { "username": "...", "password": "..." }
url = "http://example.com/?user_info=" + url_safe_encrypt(user_info)
```

Taking Things Too Far

As we said at the beginning of the chapter, our goal is to "*aggressively* identify and extract unrelated subproblems." We say "aggressively" because most coders aren't aggressive enough. But it's possible to get overexcited and take things too far.

For example, the code from the previous section could have been broken down much further, like this:

```
user_info = { "username": "...", "password": "..." }
url = "http://example.com/?user_info=" + url_safe_encrypt_obj(user_info)

def url_safe_encrypt_obj(obj):
    obj_str = json.dumps(obj)
    return url_safe_encrypt_str(obj_str)

def url_safe_encrypt_str(data):
    encrypted_bytes = encrypt(data)
    return base64.urlsafe_b64encode(encrypted_bytes)

def encrypt(data):
    cipher = make_cipher()
    encrypted_bytes = cipher.update(data)
    encrypted_bytes += cipher.final()  # flush out any remaining bytes
    return encrypted_bytes

def make_cipher():
    return Cipher("aes_128_cbc", key=PRIVATE_KEY, init_vector=INIT_VECTOR, op=ENCODE)
```

Introducing all these tiny functions actually hurts readability, because the reader has more to keep track of, and following the path of execution requires jumping around.

There is a small (but tangible) readability cost of adding a new function to your code. In the previous case, nothing is being gained to offset this cost. It may make sense to add these smaller functions if they're needed by other parts of your project. But until then, there is no need.

Summary

A simple way to think about this chapter is to **separate the generic code from the project-specific code.** As it turns out, most code is generic. By building a large set of libraries and helper functions to solve the general problems, what's left will be a small core of what makes your program unique.

The main reason this technique helps is that it lets the programmer focus on smaller, well-defined problems that are detached from the rest of your project. As a result, the solutions to those subproblems tend to be more thorough and correct. You might also be able to reuse them later.

FURTHER READING

Martin Fowler's *Refactoring: Improving the Design of Existing Code* (Fowler et al., Addison-Wesley Professional, 1999) describes the "Extract Method" of refactoring and catalogs many other ways to refactor your code.

Kent Beck's *Smalltalk Best Practice Patterns* (Prentice Hall, 1996) describes the "Composed Method Pattern," which lists a number of principles for breaking down your code into lots of little functions. In particular, one of the principles is "Keep all of the operations in a single method at the same level of abstraction."

These ideas are similar to our advice of "extracting unrelated subproblems." What we discussed in this chapter is a simple and particular case of when to extract a method.

## CHAPTER ELEVEN

One Task at a Time

Code that does multiple things at once is harder to understand. A single block of code might be initializing new objects, cleansing data, parsing inputs, and applying business logic, all at the same time. If all that code is woven together, it will be harder to understand than if each "task" is started and completed on its own.

KEY IDEA
Code should be organized so that it's doing only one task at a time.

Said another way, this chapter is about "defragmenting" your code. The following diagram illustrates this process: the left side shows the various tasks a piece of code is doing, and the right side shows that same code after it's been organized to do one task at a time.

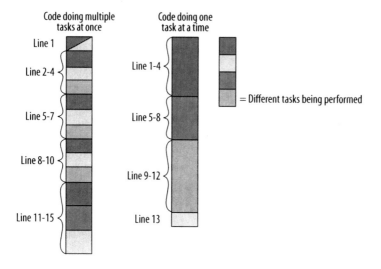

You might have heard the advice that "functions should do only one thing." Our advice is similar, but isn't always about function boundaries. Sure, breaking a large function into multiple smaller functions can be good. But even if you don't do this, you can still organize the code inside that large function so it feels like there are separate logical sections.

Here's the process we use to make code do "one task at a time":

1. List out all the "tasks" your code is doing. We use the word "task" very loosely—it could be as small as "make sure this object is valid" or as vague as "iterate through every node in the tree."

2. Try to separate those tasks as much as you can into different functions or at least different sections of code.

In this chapter, we'll show you a number of examples of how to do this.

Tasks Can Be Small

Suppose there's a voting widget on a blog where a user can vote a comment "Up" or "Down." The total score of a comment is the sum over all votes: +1 for each "Up" vote, −1 for each "Down" vote.

Here are the three states a user's vote can be in, and how it would affect the total score:

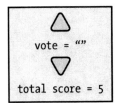

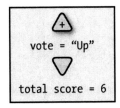

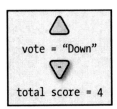

When the user clicks one of the buttons (to make/change her vote), the following JavaScript is called:

```
vote_changed(old_vote, new_vote);  // each vote is "Up", "Down", or ""
```

This function updates the total score and works for all combinations of old_vote/new_vote:

```
var vote_changed = function (old_vote, new_vote) {
    var score = get_score();

    if (new_vote !== old_vote) {
        if (new_vote === 'Up') {
            score += (old_vote === 'Down' ? 2 : 1);
        } else if (new_vote === 'Down') {
            score -= (old_vote === 'Up' ? 2 : 1);
        } else if (new_vote === '') {
            score += (old_vote === 'Up' ? -1 : 1);
        }
    }

    set_score(score);
};
```

Even though the code is pretty short, it's doing a lot. There are lots of intricate details, and it's hard to tell at a glance whether there are any off-by-one errors, typos, or other bugs.

The code may seem to be doing only one thing (updating the score), but there are actually *two* tasks being performed at once:

1. old_vote and new_vote are being "parsed" into numerical values.

2. score is being updated.

We can make the code easier to read by solving each task separately. The following code solves the first task, of parsing the vote into a numerical value:

```
var vote_value = function (vote) {
    if (vote === 'Up') {
```

```
        return +1;
    }
    if (vote === 'Down') {
        return -1;
    }
    return 0;
};
```

Now the rest of the code can solve the second task, updating score:

```
var vote_changed = function (old_vote, new_vote) {
    var score = get_score();

    score -= vote_value(old_vote);  // remove the old vote
    score += vote_value(new_vote);  // add the new vote

    set_score(score);
};
```

As you can see, this version of the code takes a lot less mental effort to convince yourself that it works. That's a big part of what makes code "easy to understand."

Extracting Values from an Object

We once had some JavaScript that formatted a user's location into a friendly string of *"City, Country"* like "Santa Monica, USA" or "Paris, France." We were given a location_info dictionary with plenty of structured information. All we had to do was pick a *"City"* and a *"Country"* from all the fields and concatenate them together.

The following illustration shows example input/output:

location_info

LocalityName	"Santa Monica"
SubAdministrativeAreaName	"Los Angeles"
AdministrativeAreaName	"California"
CountryName	"USA"

"Santa Monica, USA"

It seems easy so far, but the tricky part is that *any or all of these four values might be missing.* Here's how we dealt with that:

- When choosing the "City," we preferred to use the "LocalityName" (city/town) if available, then the "SubAdministrativeAreaName" (larger city/county), then the "AdministrativeAreaName" (state/territory).

- If all three were missing, the "City" was affectionately given the default "Middle-of-Nowhere."
- If the "CountryName" was missing, "Planet Earth" was used as a default.

The following figure shows two examples of handling missing values.

location_info

LocalityName	(undefined)
SubAdministrativeAreaName	(undefined)
AdministrativeAreaName	(undefined)
CountryName	"Canada"

⬇

"Middle-of-Nowhere, Canada"

location_info

LocalityName	(undefined)
SubAdministrativeAreaName	"Washington, DC"
AdministrativeAreaName	(undefined)
CountryName	"USA"

⬇

"Washington, DC, USA"

Here is the code we wrote to implement this task:

```
var place = location_info["LocalityName"];  // e.g. "Santa Monica"
if (!place) {
    place = location_info["SubAdministrativeAreaName"];  // e.g. "Los Angeles"
}
if (!place) {
    place = location_info["AdministrativeAreaName"];  // e.g. "California"
}
if (!place) {
    place = "Middle-of-Nowhere";
}
if (location_info["CountryName"]) {
    place += ", " + location_info["CountryName"];  // e.g. "USA"
} else {
    place += ", Planet Earth";
}

return place;
```

Sure, it's a little messy, but it got the job done.

But a few days later, we needed to improve the functionality: for locations in the United States, we wanted to display the *state* instead of the country (if possible). So instead of "Santa Monica, USA" it would return "Santa Monica, California."

Adding this feature to the previous code would have made it much uglier.

Applying "One Task at a Time"

Rather than bend this code to our will, we stopped and realized that it was already doing multiple tasks at the same time:

1. Extracting values from the dictionary `location_info`

2. Going through a preference order for "City," defaulting to "Middle-of-Nowhere" if it couldn't find anything

3. Getting the "Country," and using "Planet Earth" if there wasn't one

4. Updating place

So instead, we rewrote the original code to solve each of these tasks independently.

The first task (extracting values from `location_info`) was easy to solve on its own:

```
var town    = location_info["LocalityName"];              // e.g. "Santa Monica"
var city    = location_info["SubAdministrativeAreaName"]; // e.g. "Los Angeles"
var state   = location_info["AdministrativeAreaName"];    // e.g. "CA"
var country = location_info["CountryName"];               // e.g. "USA"
```

At this point, we were done using `location_info` and didn't have to remember those long and unintuitive keys. Instead, we had four simple variables to work with.

Next, we had to figure out what the "second half" of the return value would be:

```
// Start with the default, and keep overwriting with the most specific value.
var second_half = "Planet Earth";
if (country) {
    second_half = country;
}
if (state && country === "USA") {
    second_half = state;
}
```

Similarly, we could figure out the "first half":

```
var first_half = "Middle-of-Nowhere";
if (state && country !== "USA") {
    first_half = state;
}
if (city) {
    first_half = city;
}
if (town) {
    first_half = town;
}
```

Finally, we pieced the information together:

```
return first_half + ", " + second_half;
```

The "defragmentation" illustration at the beginning of this chapter was actually a representation of the original solution and this new version. Here's that same illustration, with more details filled in:

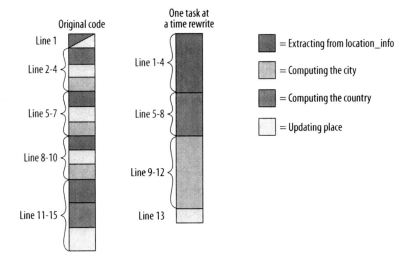

Original code

Line 1
Line 2-4
Line 5-7
Line 8-10
Line 11-15

One task at
a time rewrite

Line 1-4
Line 5-8
Line 9-12
Line 13

■ = Extracting from location_info
□ = Computing the city
■ = Computing the country
□ = Updating place

As you can see, the four tasks in the second solution have been defragmented into distinct regions.

Another Approach

When refactoring code, there are often multiple ways to do it, and this case is no exception. Once you've separated some of the tasks, the code gets easier to think about, and you might come up with even better ways to refactor it.

For instance, that earlier series of if statements requires some careful reading to know if every case works correctly. There are actually two subtasks going on simultaneously in that code:

1. Go through a list of variables, and pick the most preferred one that's available.
2. Use a different list, depending on whether the country is "USA".

Looking back, you can see that the earlier code has the "if USA" logic interwoven with the rest of the logic. Instead, we can handle the USA and non-USA cases separately:

```
var first_half, second_half;

if (country === "USA") {
    first_half = town || city || "Middle-of-Nowhere";
    second_half = state || "USA";
} else {
    first_half = town || city || state || "Middle-of-Nowhere";
    second_half = country || "Planet Earth";
}

return first_half + ", " + second_half;
```

In case you aren't familiar with JavaScript, a || b || c is idiomatic and evaluates to the first "truthy" value (in this case, a defined, nonempty string). This code has the benefit that it's very easy to inspect the preference list and update it. Most of the if statements have been swept away, and the business logic is represented by fewer lines of code.

A Larger Example

In a web-crawling system we built, a function named UpdateCounts() was called to increment various statistics after each web page was downloaded:

```
void UpdateCounts(HttpDownload hd) {
    counts["Exit State"   ][hd.exit_state()]++;      // e.g. "SUCCESS" or "FAILURE"
    counts["Http Response"][hd.http_response()]++;   // e.g. "404 NOT FOUND"
    counts["Content-Type" ][hd.content_type()]++;    // e.g. "text/html"
}
```

Well, that's how we *wish* the code looked!

In actuality, the HttpDownload object had none of the methods shown here. Instead, HttpDownload was a very large and complex class, with many nested classes, and we had to fish out those values ourselves. To make matters worse, sometimes those values were missing altogether—in which case we just used "unknown" as the default value.

Because of all this, the real code was quite a mess:

```
// WARNING: DO NOT STARE DIRECTLY AT THIS CODE FOR EXTENDED PERIODS OF TIME.
void UpdateCounts(HttpDownload hd) {
    // Figure out the Exit State, if available.
    if (!hd.has_event_log() || !hd.event_log().has_exit_state()) {
        counts["Exit State"]["unknown"]++;
    } else {
        string state_str = ExitStateTypeName(hd.event_log().exit_state());
        counts["Exit State"][state_str]++;
    }

    // If there are no HTTP headers at all, use "unknown" for the remaining elements.
    if (!hd.has_http_headers()) {
        counts["Http Response"]["unknown"]++;
        counts["Content-Type"]["unknown"]++;
        return;
    }

    HttpHeaders headers = hd.http_headers();

    // Log the HTTP response, if known, otherwise log "unknown"
    if (!headers.has_response_code()) {
        counts["Http Response"]["unknown"]++;
    } else {
        string code = StringPrintf("%d", headers.response_code());
        counts["Http Response"][code]++;
    }

    // Log the Content-Type if known, otherwise log "unknown"
    if (!headers.has_content_type()) {
        counts["Content-Type"]["unknown"]++;
```

```
    } else {
        string content_type = ContentTypeMime(headers.content_type());
        counts["Content-Type"][content_type]++;
    }
}
```

As you can see, there's a lot of code, and a lot of logic, and even a few repeated lines of code. This code is not fun to read.

In particular, this code switches back and forth between different tasks. Here are the different tasks interleaved throughout the code:

1. Using "unknown" as the default value for each key

2. Detecting whether members of HttpDownload are missing

3. Extracting the value and converting it to a string

4. Updating counts[]

We can improve the code by separating some of these tasks into distinct regions in the code:

```
void UpdateCounts(HttpDownload hd) {
    // Task: define default values for each of the values we want to extract
    string exit_state = "unknown";
    string http_response = "unknown";
    string content_type = "unknown";

    // Task: try to extract each value from HttpDownload, one by one
    if (hd.has_event_log() && hd.event_log().has_exit_state()) {
        exit_state = ExitStateTypeName(hd.event_log().exit_state());
    }
    if (hd.has_http_headers() && hd.http_headers().has_response_code()) {
        http_response = StringPrintf("%d", hd.http_headers().response_code());
    }
    if (hd.has_http_headers() && hd.http_headers().has_content_type()) {
        content_type = ContentTypeMime(hd.http_headers().content_type());
    }

    // Task: update counts[]
    counts["Exit State"][exit_state]++;
    counts["Http Response"][http_response]++;
    counts["Content-Type"][content_type]++;
}
```

As you can see, the code has three separate regions with the following aims:

1. Define defaults for the three keys we are interested in.

2. Extract the values, if available, for each of these keys, and convert them to strings.

3. Update counts[] for each key/value.

What's good about these regions is that they're *isolated* from one another—while you're reading one region, you don't need to think about the other regions.

Note that although we listed four tasks, we were able to separate only three of them. That's perfectly fine: the tasks you list initially are just a starting point. Even separating *some* of them can help things a lot, as it did here.

Further Improvements

This new version of the code is a marked improvement from the original monstrosity. And notice that we didn't even have to create other functions to perform this cleanup. As we mentioned before, the idea of "one task at a time" can help you clean up code regardless of function boundaries.

However, we could also have improved this code another way, by introducing three helper functions:

```
void UpdateCounts(HttpDownload hd) {
    counts["Exit State"][ExitState(hd)]++;
    counts["Http Response"][HttpResponse(hd)]++;
    counts["Content-Type"][ContentType(hd)]++;
}
```

These functions would extract the corresponding value, or return "unknown". For example:

```
string ExitState(HttpDownload hd) {
    if (hd.has_event_log() && hd.event_log().has_exit_state()) {
        return ExitStateTypeName(hd.event_log().exit_state());
    } else {
        return "unknown";
    }
}
```

Notice that this alternative solution doesn't even define any variables! As we mentioned in Chapter 9, *Variables and Readability*, variables that hold intermediate results can often be eliminated entirely.

In this solution, we've simply "sliced" the problem in a different direction. Both solutions are highly readable, as they require the reader to think about only one task at a time.

Summary

This chapter illustrates a simple technique for organizing your code: **do only one task at a time**.

If you have code that's difficult to read, try to list all of the tasks it's doing. Some of these tasks might easily become separate functions (or classes). Others might just become logical "paragraphs" within a single function. The exact details of how you separate these tasks isn't as important as the fact that they're separated. The hard part is accurately describing all the little things your program is doing.

## CHAPTER TWELVE

Turning Thoughts into Code

> You do not really understand something unless you can explain it to your grandmother.
>
> —Albert Einstein

When explaining a complex idea to someone, it's easy to confuse them with all the little details. It's a valuable skill to be able to explain an idea "in plain English," so that someone less knowledgeable than you can understand. It requires distilling an idea down to the most important concepts. Doing this not only helps the other person understand but also helps you think about your own ideas more clearly.

The same skill should be used when "presenting" code to your reader. We take the view that source code is the primary way to explain what a program is doing. So the code should be written "in plain English."

In this chapter, we'll use a simple process that can help you code more clearly:

1. Describe what code needs to do, in plain English, as you would to a colleague.

2. Pay attention to the key words and phrases used in this description.

3. Write your code to match this description.

Describing Logic Clearly

Here is a snippet of code from a web page in PHP. This code is at the top of a secured page. It checks whether the user is authorized to see the page, and if not, immediately returns a page telling the user she is not authorized:

```php
$is_admin = is_admin_request();
if ($document) {
    if (!$is_admin && ($document['username'] != $_SESSION['username'])) {
        return not_authorized();
    }
} else {
    if (!$is_admin) {
        return not_authorized();
    }
}

// continue rendering the page ...
```

There's quite a bit of logic in this code. As you saw in Part II, *Simplifying Loops and Logic*, large logic trees like this aren't easy to understand. The logic in this code can probably be simplified, but how? Let's start by describing the logic in plain English:

```
There are two ways you can be authorized:
1) you are an admin
2) you own the current document (if there is one)
Otherwise, you are not authorized.
```

Here is an alternative solution inspired by this description:

```
if (is_admin_request()) {
    // authorized
} elseif ($document && ($document['username'] == $_SESSION['username'])) {
    // authorized
} else {
    return not_authorized();
}

// continue rendering the page ...
```

This version is slightly unusual because it has two empty bodies. But the code is smaller, and the logic is simpler, because there is no negation. (The previous solution had three "nots.") The bottom line is that it's easier to understand.

Knowing Your Libraries Helps

We once had a website that included a "tips box" that showed the user helpful suggestions like:

```
Tip: Log in to see your past queries. [Show me another tip!]
```

There were a few dozen tips, and all of them were hidden inside the HTML:

```
<div id="tip-1" class="tip">Tip: Log in to see your past queries.</div>
<div id="tip-2" class="tip">Tip: Click on a picture to see it close up.</div>
...
```

When a user visited the page, one of these divs was randomly made visible, and the rest stayed hidden.

If the "Show me another tip!" link was clicked, it cycled to the next tip. Here is some code to implement that feature using the jQuery JavaScript library:

```
var show_next_tip = function () {
    var num_tips = $('.tip').size();
    var shown_tip = $('.tip:visible');

    var shown_tip_num = Number(shown_tip.attr('id').slice(4));
    if (shown_tip_num === num_tips) {
        $('#tip-1').show();
    } else {
        $('#tip-' + (shown_tip_num + 1)).show();
    }
    shown_tip.hide();
};
```

This code is okay. But it can be made better. Let's start by describing, in words, what this code is trying to do:

```
Find the currently visible tip and hide it.
Then find the next tip after it and show that.
If we've run out of tips, cycle back to the first tip.
```

Based on this description, here's another solution:

```
var show_next_tip = function () {
    var cur_tip = $('.tip:visible').hide();  // find the currently visible tip and hide it
    var next_tip = cur_tip.next('.tip');     // find the next tip after it
    if (next_tip.size() === 0) {             // if we've run out of tips,
        next_tip = $('.tip:first');          //     cycle back to the first tip
    }
    next_tip.show();                         // show the new tip
};
```

This solution contains fewer lines of code and doesn't have to manipulate integers directly. It's more aligned with how a person would think about the code.

In this case, it helped that jQuery has a .next() method we could use. Part of writing succinct code is being aware of what your library has to offer.

Applying This Method to Larger Problems

The previous examples have applied our process to small blocks of code. In the next example, we'll apply it to a larger function. As you'll see, this method can help you break down your code by helping you identify what pieces you can break away.

Imagine we have a system that records stock purchases. Each transaction has four pieces of data:

- time (a precise date and time of the purchase)
- ticker_symbol (e.g., GOOG)
- price (e.g., $600)
- number_of_shares (e.g., 100)

For some strange reason, the data is spread across three separate database tables, as illustrated here. In each database, the time is the unique primary key.

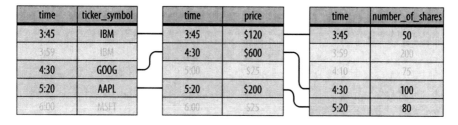

time	ticker_symbol		time	price		time	number_of_shares
3:45	IBM		3:45	$120		3:45	50
3:59	IBM		4:30	$600		3:59	200
4:30	GOOG		5:00	$25		4:10	75
5:20	AAPL		5:20	$200		4:30	100
6:00	MSFT		6:00	$25		5:20	80

Now we need to write a program to join the three tables back together (as an SQL JOIN operation would do). This step should be easy because the rows are all sorted by time, but unfortunately some of the rows are missing. You want to find all the rows where all three times match up, and ignore any rows that can't be lined up, as shown in the previous illustration.

Here is some Python code that finds all the matching rows:

```python
def PrintStockTransactions():
    stock_iter = db_read("SELECT time, ticker_symbol FROM ...")
    price_iter = ...
    num_shares_iter = ...

    # Iterate through all the rows of the 3 tables in parallel.
    while stock_iter and price_iter and num_shares_iter:
        stock_time = stock_iter.time
        price_time = price_iter.time
        num_shares_time = num_shares_iter.time

        # If all 3 rows don't have the same time, skip over the oldest row
        # Note: the "<=" below can't just be "<" in case there are 2 tied-oldest.
        if stock_time != price_time or stock_time != num_shares_time:
            if stock_time <= price_time and stock_time <= num_shares_time:
                stock_iter.NextRow()
            elif price_time <= stock_time and price_time <= num_shares_time:
                price_iter.NextRow()
            elif num_shares_time <= stock_time and num_shares_time <= price_time:
                num_shares_iter.NextRow()
            else:
                assert False  # impossible
            continue

        assert stock_time == price_time == num_shares_time

        # Print the aligned rows.
        print "@", stock_time,
        print stock_iter.ticker_symbol,
        print price_iter.price,
        print num_shares_iter.number_of_shares

        stock_iter.NextRow()
        price_iter.NextRow()
        num_shares_iter.NextRow()
```

This example code works, but there's a lot going on with how the loop skips over unmatched rows. Some warning flags might have gone off in your head: *Could this miss any rows? Might it read past the end-of-stream for any of the iterators?*

So how can we make it more readable?

An English Description of the Solution

Once again, let's step back and describe in plain English what we're trying to do:

```
We are reading three row iterators in parallel.
Whenever the rows' times don't line up, advance the rows so they do line up.
Then print the aligned rows, and advance the rows again.
Keep doing this until there are no more matching rows left.
```

Looking back at the original code, the messiest part was the block dealing with "advance the rows so they do line up." To present the code more clearly, we can extract all that messy logic into a new function named AdvanceToMatchingTime().

Here's a new version of the code, making use of this new function:

```python
def PrintStockTransactions():
    stock_iter = ...
    price_iter = ...
    num_shares_iter = ...

    while True:
        time = AdvanceToMatchingTime(stock_iter, price_iter, num_shares_iter)
        if time is None:
            return

        # Print the aligned rows.
        print "@", time,
        print stock_iter.ticker_symbol,
        print price_iter.price,
        print num_shares_iter.number_of_shares

        stock_iter.NextRow()
        price_iter.NextRow()
        num_shares_iter.NextRow()
```

As you can see, this code is much easier to understand, as we've hidden away all the dirty details of lining up the rows.

Applying the Method Recursively

It's easy to imagine how you would write AdvanceToMatchingTime()—in the worst case, it would look very similar to that ugly block of code from the first version:

```python
def AdvanceToMatchingTime(stock_iter, price_iter, num_shares_iter):
    # Iterate through all the rows of the 3 tables in parallel.
    while stock_iter and price_iter and num_shares_iter:
        stock_time = stock_iter.time
        price_time = price_iter.time
        num_shares_time = num_shares_iter.time

        # If all 3 rows don't have the same time, skip over the oldest row
        if stock_time != price_time or stock_time != num_shares_time:
            if stock_time <= price_time and stock_time <= num_shares_time:
                stock_iter.NextRow()
            elif price_time <= stock_time and price_time <= num_shares_time:
                price_iter.NextRow()
            elif num_shares_time <= stock_time and num_shares_time <= price_time:
                num_shares_iter.NextRow()
            else:
                assert False  # impossible
            continue
```

```
        assert stock_time == price_time == num_shares_time
        return stock_time
```

But let's improve that code by applying our method to `AdvanceToMatchingTime()` as well. Here's a description of what this function needs to do:

```
Look at the times of each current row: if they're aligned, we're done.
Otherwise, advance any rows that are "behind."
Keep doing this until the rows are aligned (or one of the iterators has ended).
```

This description is a lot clearer and more elegant than the previous code. One thing to notice is that the description never mentions `stock_iter` or other details specific to our problem. This means we can also rename the variables to be simpler and more general. Here's the resulting code:

```
def AdvanceToMatchingTime(row_iter1, row_iter2, row_iter3):
    while row_iter1 and row_iter2 and row_iter3:
        t1 = row_iter1.time
        t2 = row_iter2.time
        t3 = row_iter3.time

        if t1 == t2 == t3:
            return t1

        tmax = max(t1, t2, t3)

        # If any row is "behind," advance it.
        # Eventually, this while loop will align them all.
        if t1 < tmax: row_iter1.NextRow()
        if t2 < tmax: row_iter2.NextRow()
        if t3 < tmax: row_iter3.NextRow()

    return None  # no alignment could be found
```

As you can see, this code is a lot clearer than before. The algorithm became simpler, and now there are fewer tricky comparisons. And we used short names like t1 and no longer had to think about the specific database columns involved.

Summary

This chapter discussed the simple technique of describing your program in plain English and using that description to help you write more natural code. This technique is deceptively simple, but very powerful. Looking at the words and phrases used in your description can also help you identify which subproblems to break off.

But this process of "saying things in plain English" is applicable outside of just writing code. For example, one college computer lab policy states that when a student needs help debugging his program, he first has to explain the problem to a dedicated teddy bear in the corner of the room. Surprisingly, just describing the problem aloud can often help the student figure out a solution. This technique is called "rubber ducking."

Another way to look at it is this: if you can't describe the problem or your design in words, something is probably missing or undefined. Getting a program (or any idea) into words can really force it into shape.

## CHAPTER THIRTEEN

Writing Less Code

Knowing when *not* to code is possibly the most important skill a programmer can learn. Every line of code you write is a line that has to be tested and maintained. By reusing libraries or eliminating features, you can save time and keep your codebase lean and mean.

KEY IDEA
The most readable code is no code at all.

Don't Bother Implementing That Feature—You Won't Need It

When you start a project, it's natural to get excited and think of all the cool features you'll want to implement. But programmers tend to overestimate how many features are *truly essential* to their project. A lot of features go unfinished or unused or just complicate the application.

Programmers also tend to underestimate how much effort it takes to implement a feature. We optimistically estimate how long it will take to implement a crude prototype but forget how much extra time is involved in future maintenance, documentation, and the added "weight" to the codebase.

Question and Break Down Your Requirements

Not all programs need to be fast, 100% correct, and able to handle every possible input. If you really scrutinize your requirements, sometimes you can carve out a simpler problem that requires less code. Let's look at some examples of this.

Example: A Store Locator

Suppose you were writing a "store locator" for a business. You think your requirements are:

> For any given user's latitude/longitude, find the store with the closest latitude/longitude.

To implement this 100% correctly, you would need to handle:

- When the locations are on either side of the International Date Line
- When the locations are near the North or South Pole
- Adjusting for the curvature of the Earth, as "longitudinal degrees per mile" changes

Handling all of these cases requires a fair amount of code.

For your application, however, there are only 30 stores in the state of Texas. In this smaller region, the three issues in the list aren't that important. As a result, you can reduce your requirements to:

> For a user near Texas, find (approximately) the closest store in Texas.

Solving this problem is easier, as you can get away with just iterating through each store and computing the Euclidean distance between the latitudes/longitudes.

Example: Adding a Cache

We once had a Java application that frequently read objects from disk. The speed of the application was limited by these reads, so we wanted to implement caching of some sort. A typical sequence of reads looked like this:

```
read Object A
read Object A
read Object A
read Object B
read Object B
read Object C
read Object D
read Object D
```

As you can see, there were a lot of repeated accesses to the same object, so caching should definitely have helped.

When faced with this problem, our first instinct was to use a cache that discards the least recently used items. We didn't have one available in our library, so we would have had to implement it ourselves. That wasn't a problem though, as we've implemented such a data structure before (it involves both a hash table and a singly linked list—perhaps 100 lines of code in total).

However, we noticed that the repeated accesses were always in a row. So instead of implementing an LRU cache, we just implemented a one-item cache:

```
DiskObject lastUsed;  // class member

DiskObject lookUp(String key) {
    if (lastUsed == null || !lastUsed.key().equals(key)) {
        lastUsed = loadDiskObject(key);
    }

    return lastUsed;
}
```

This got us 90% of the benefit without much coding, and the program had a small memory footprint, too.

The benefits of "removing requirements" and "solving simpler problems" can't be overstated. Requirements often interfere with each other in subtle ways. This means that solving half the problem might only take a quarter as much coding effort.

Keeping Your Codebase Small

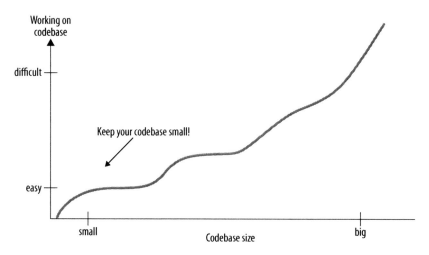

When you first start a software project, and you have only one or two source files, things are great. Compiling and running the code is a snap, it's easy to make changes, and it's easy to remember where each function or class is defined.

Then, as the project grows, your directory fills up with more and more source files. Soon you need multiple directories to organize them all. It's harder to remember which functions call which other functions, and tracking down bugs takes a little more work.

Eventually, you have lots of source code spread across many different directories. The project is huge, and no single person understands it all. Adding new features becomes painful, and working with the code is cumbersome and unpleasant.

What we've described is a natural law of the universe—as any coordinated system grows, the complexity needed to keep it glued together grows even faster.

The best way to cope is to **keep your codebase as small and lightweight as possible**, even as your project grows. Thus you should:

- Create as much generic "utility" code as possible to remove duplicated code. (See Chapter 10, *Extracting Unrelated Subproblems*.)
- Remove unused code or useless features. (See the following sidebar.)
- Keep your project compartmentalized into disconnected subprojects.
- Generally, be conscious of the "weight" of your codebase. Keep it light and nimble.

REMOVING UNUSED CODE

Gardeners often prune plants to keep them alive and growing. Similarly, it's a good idea to prune any unused code that's getting in the way.

Once code is written, coders are often reluctant to delete it, because it represents a lot of real work. To delete it would mean admitting that the time spent on it was wasted. Well, get over it! This is a creative field—photographers, writers, and filmmakers don't keep all of their work, either.

Deleting isolated functions is easy, but sometimes "unused code" is actually woven throughout your project, unbeknownst to you. Here are some examples:

- You originally designed your system to handle international filenames, and now the code is littered with conversion code. However, that code isn't fully functional, and your app is never used with international filenames anyhow.

  Why not remove this functionality?

- You wanted your program to work even if the system ran out of memory, so you have lots of clever logic that tries to recover from out-of-memory situations. It was a good idea, but in practice, when the system runs out of memory, your program just becomes an unstable zombie anyway—all the core features are unusable, and it's one mouse click away from dying.

  Why not just terminate the program with a simple "The system is out of memory, sorry" and remove all this out-of-memory code?

Be Familiar with the Libraries Around You

A lot of the time, programmers just aren't aware that existing libraries can solve their problem. Or sometimes they've forgotten what a library can do. It's important to know the capabilities of your library code so that you can make use of it.

Here's a modest suggestion: **every once in a while, spend 15 minutes reading the names of all the functions/modules/types in your standard library.** These include the C++ Standard Template Library (STL), the Java API, the built-in Python modules, and others.

The goal isn't to memorize the whole library. It's just to get a sense of what's available, so that next time you're working on new code you'll think, "Wait, this sounds similar to something I saw in the API...." We believe doing this work upfront pays off quickly, as you'll be more inclined to use those libraries in the first place.

Example: Lists and Sets in Python

Suppose you have a list in Python (like [2,1,2]) and you want a list of the unique elements (in this case, [2,1]). You could implement this task using a dictionary, which has a list of keys that are guaranteed to be unique:

```
def unique(elements):
    temp = {}
    for element in elements:
        temp[element] = None  # The value doesn't matter.
    return temp.keys()

unique_elements = unique([2,1,2])
```

But instead you can just use the lesser-known set type:

```
unique_elements = set([2,1,2])  # Remove duplicates
```

This object is iterable, just like a normal list. If you really want a list object again, you can just use:

```
unique_elements = list(set([2,1,2]))  # Remove duplicates
```

Clearly, set is the right tool for the job here. But if you weren't aware of the set type, you might produce code like unique() above.

Why Reusing Libraries Is Such a Win

A commonly cited statistic is that the average software engineer produces ten shippable lines of code a day. When programmers first hear this, they balk in disbelief—"Ten lines of code? I can write that in a minute!"

The key word is *shippable*. Each line of code in a mature library represents a fair amount of design, debugging, rewriting, documenting, optimizing, and testing. Any line of code that's survived this Darwinian process is very valuable. This is why reusing libraries is such a win, in both saving time and having less code to write.

Example: Using Unix Tools Instead of Coding

When a web server frequently returns 4xx or 5xx HTTP response codes, it's a sign of a potential problem (4xx being a client error; 5xx being a server error). So we wanted to write a program that parses a web server's access logs and determines which URLs are causing the most errors.

The access logs typically look something like this:

```
1.2.3.4 example.com [24/Aug/2010:01:08:34] "GET /index.html HTTP/1.1" 200 ...
2.3.4.5 example.com [24/Aug/2010:01:14:27] "GET /help?topic=8 HTTP/1.1" 500 ...
3.4.5.6 example.com [24/Aug/2010:01:15:54] "GET /favicon.ico HTTP/1.1" 404 ...
...
```

Generally, they contain lines of this form:

```
browser-IP host [date] "GET /url-path HTTP/1.1" HTTP-response-code ...
```

Writing a program to find the most common url-paths with 4xx or 5xx response codes might easily take 20 lines of code in a language like C++ or Java.

Instead, in Unix, you can type this command line:

```
cat access.log | awk '{ print $5 " " $7 }' | egrep "[45]..$" \
| sort | uniq -c | sort -nr
```

which produces output like this:

```
95 /favicon.ico 404
13 /help?topic=8 500
11 /login 403
...
<count> <path> <http response code>
```

What's great about this command line is that we've avoided writing any "real" code or checking anything into source control.

Summary

> Adventure, excitement—a Jedi craves not these things.
>
> —Yoda

This chapter is about writing as little new code as possible. Each new line of code needs to be tested, documented, and maintained. Further, the more code in your codebase, the "heavier" it gets and the harder it is to develop in.

You can avoid writing new lines of code by:

- Eliminating nonessential features from your product and not overengineering
- Rethinking requirements to solve the easiest version of the problem that still gets the job done
- Staying familiar with standard libraries by periodically reading through their entire APIs

Selected Topics

In the previous three parts, we covered a wide range of techniques for making code easy to understand. In this part, we're going to apply some of these techniques to two selected topics.

First, we're going to discuss testing—how to write tests that are effective and readable at the same time.

Then we're going to walk through the design and implementation of a special-purpose data structure (a "minute/hour counter") to see an example where performance, good design, and readability interplay.

## CHAPTER FOURTEEN

Testing and Readability

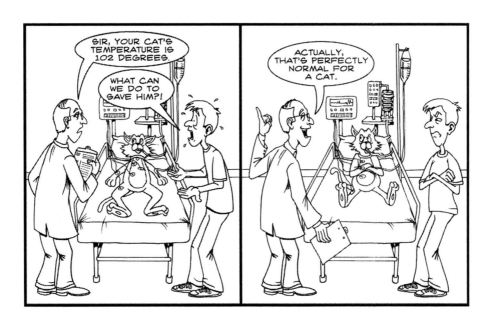

In this chapter, we're going to show you simple techniques to write neat and effective tests.

Testing means different things to different people. In this chapter, we use "test" to mean *any* code whose sole purpose is to check the behavior of another ("real") piece of code. We're going to focus on the readability aspect of tests and not get into whether you should write test code before writing real code ("test-driven development") or other philosophical aspects of test development.

Make Tests Easy to Read and Maintain

It's just as important for test code to be readable as it is for nontest code. Other coders will often look at the test code as unofficial documentation of how the real code works and should be used. So if the tests are easy to read, users will better understand how the real code behaves.

> **KEY IDEA**
> **Test code should be readable so that other coders are comfortable changing or adding tests.**

When test code is big and scary, here's what happens:

- **Coders are afraid to modify the real code.** *Oh, we don't want to mess with that code— updating all the tests would be a nightmare!*
- **Coders don't add new tests** when they add new code. Over time, less and less of your module is tested, and you are no longer confident that it all works.

Instead, you want to encourage users of your code (especially you!) to be comfortable with the test code. They should be able to diagnose why a new change is breaking an existing test and feel like adding new tests is easy.

What's Wrong with This Test?

In our codebase, we had a function to sort and filter a list of scored search results. Here's the function declaration:

```
// Sort 'docs' by score (highest first) and remove negative-scored documents.
void SortAndFilterDocs(vector<ScoredDocument>* docs);
```

The test for this function originally looked something like:

```
void Test1() {
    vector<ScoredDocument> docs;
    docs.resize(5);
    docs[0].url = "http://example.com";
    docs[0].score = -5.0;
    docs[1].url = "http://example.com";
    docs[1].score = 1;
```

```
    docs[2].url = "http://example.com";
    docs[2].score = 4;
    docs[3].url = "http://example.com";
    docs[3].score = -99998.7;
    docs[4].url = "http://example.com";
    docs[4].score = 3.0;

    SortAndFilterDocs(&docs);

    assert(docs.size() == 3);
    assert(docs[0].score == 4);
    assert(docs[1].score == 3.0);
    assert(docs[2].score == 1);
}
```

There are at least *eight* different problems with this test code. By the end of the chapter, you'll be able to identify and fix all of them.

Making This Test More Readable

As a general design principle, you should **hide less important details from the user, so that more important details are most prominent.**

The test code from the previous section clearly violates this principle. Every detail of the test is front and center, like the unimportant minutiae of setting up a vector<ScoredDocument>. Most of the example code involves url, score, and docs[], which are just details about how the underlying C++ objects are set up, not about what this test is doing at a high level.

As a first step in cleaning this up, we could create a helper function like:

```
void MakeScoredDoc(ScoredDocument* sd, double score, string url) {
    sd->score = score;
    sd->url = url;
}
```

Using this function, our test code becomes slightly more compact:

```
void Test1() {
    vector<ScoredDocument> docs;
    docs.resize(5);
    MakeScoredDoc(&docs[0], -5.0, "http://example.com");
    MakeScoredDoc(&docs[1], 1, "http://example.com");
    MakeScoredDoc(&docs[2], 4, "http://example.com");
    MakeScoredDoc(&docs[3], -99998.7, "http://example.com");
    ...
}
```

But this isn't good enough—there are still unimportant details in our face. For instance, the parameter "http://example.com" is just an eyesore. It's always the same, and the exact URL doesn't even matter—it's just needed to fill out a valid ScoredDocument.

Another unimportant detail we're forced to see is docs.resize(5) and &docs[0], &docs[1], and so on. Let's change our helper function to do more work for us and call it AddScoredDoc():

```
void AddScoredDoc(vector<ScoredDocument>& docs, double score) {
    ScoredDocument sd;
    sd.score = score;
    sd.url = "http://example.com";
    docs.push_back(sd);
}
```

Using this function, our test code is even more compact:

```
void Test1() {
    vector<ScoredDocument> docs;
    AddScoredDoc(docs, -5.0);
    AddScoredDoc(docs, 1);
    AddScoredDoc(docs, 4);
    AddScoredDoc(docs, -99998.7);
    ...
}
```

This code is better, but still doesn't pass the "highly readable and writable" test. If you wanted to add another test with a new set of scored docs, it would require a lot of copying and pasting. So how do we go about improving it further?

Creating the Minimal Test Statement

To improve this test code, let's use the technique from Chapter 12, *Turning Thoughts into Code*. Let's describe what our test is trying to do in plain English:

> We have a list of documents whose scores are [-5, 1, 4, -99998.7, 3]. After SortAndFilterDocs(), the remaining documents should have scores of [4, 3, 1], in that order.

As you can see, nowhere in that description did we mention a vector<ScoredDocument>. The array of scores is what's most important here. Ideally, our test code would look something like:

```
CheckScoresBeforeAfter("-5, 1, 4, -99998.7, 3",  "4, 3, 1");
```

We were able to boil the essence of this test down to one line of code!

This is not uncommon, though. The essence of most tests boils down to *for this input/situation, expect this behavior/output*. And many times this goal can be expressed in just one line. In addition to making the code very compact and readable, keeping your test statements short makes it very easy to add more test cases.

Implementing Custom "Minilanguages"

Notice that CheckScoresBeforeAfter() takes two string arguments that describe the array of scores. In later versions of C++, you can pass in array literals like this:

```
CheckScoresBeforeAfter({-5, 1, 4, -99998.7, 3}, {4, 3, 1});
```

Because we couldn't do this at the time, we put the scores inside a string, separated by commas. For this approach to work, CheckScoresBeforeAfter() is going to have to parse those string arguments.

In general, defining a custom minilanguage can be a powerful way to express a lot of information in a small amount of space. Other examples include printf() and regular expression libraries.

In this case, writing some helper functions to parse a comma-separated list of numbers shouldn't be too hard. Here's what CheckScoresBeforeAfter() would look like:

```
void CheckScoresBeforeAfter(string input, string expected_output) {
    vector<ScoredDocument> docs = ScoredDocsFromString(input);
    SortAndFilterDocs(&docs);
    string output = ScoredDocsToString(docs);
    assert(output == expected_output);
}
```

And for completeness, here are the helper functions that convert between string and vector<ScoredDocument>:

```
vector<ScoredDocument> ScoredDocsFromString(string scores) {
    vector<ScoredDocument> docs;

    replace(scores.begin(), scores.end(), ',', ' ');

    // Populate 'docs' from a string of space-separated scores.
    istringstream stream(scores);
    double score;
    while (stream >> score) {
        AddScoredDoc(docs, score);
    }

    return docs;
}

string ScoredDocsToString(vector<ScoredDocument> docs) {
    ostringstream stream;
    for (int i = 0; i < docs.size(); i++) {
        if (i > 0) stream << ", ";
        stream << docs[i].score;
    }

    return stream.str();
}
```

This may seem like a lot of code at first glance, but what it lets you do is incredibly powerful. Because you can write an entire test with just one call to CheckScoresBeforeAfter(), you'll be inclined to add more tests (as we'll be doing later in the chapter).

Making Error Messages Readable

The preceding code was nice, but what happens when that assert(output == expected_output) line fails? It produces an error message like this:

```
Assertion failed: (output == expected_output),
    function CheckScoresBeforeAfter, file test.cc, line 37.
```

Obviously, if you ever saw this error, you'd wonder, *What were the values of* output *and* expected_output*?*

Using Better Versions of assert()

Fortunately, most languages and libraries have more sophisticated versions of assert() you can use. So instead of writing:

```
assert(output == expected_output);
```

you could use the Boost C++ library:

```
BOOST_REQUIRE_EQUAL(output, expected_output)
```

Now, if the test fails, you get a more detailed message like:

```
test.cc(37): fatal error in "CheckScoresBeforeAfter": critical check
    output == expected_output failed ["1, 3, 4" != "4, 3, 1"]
```

which is much more helpful.

You should use these more helpful assertion methods when they're available. It'll pay off every time your test fails.

BETTER ASSERT() IN OTHER LANGUAGES

In Python, the built-in statement assert a == b produces a plain error message like:

```
File "file.py", line X, in <module>
    assert a == b
AssertionError
```

Instead, you can use the assertEqual() method in the unittest module:

```
import unittest

class MyTestCase(unittest.TestCase):
    def testFunction(self):
        a = 1
        b = 2
        self.assertEqual(a, b)

if __name__ == '__main__':
    unittest.main()
```

which produces an error message like:

```
File "MyTestCase.py", line 7, in testFunction
        self.assertEqual(a, b)
AssertionError: 1 != 2
```

Whichever language you're using, there's probably a library/framework (e.g., XUnit) available to help you. It pays to know your libraries!

Hand-Crafted Error Messages

Using BOOST_REQUIRE_EQUAL(), we were able to get the nicer error message:

```
output == expected_output failed ["1, 3, 4" != "4, 3, 1"]
```

However, this message could be improved further. For instance, it would be useful to see the original input that triggered this failure. The ideal error message would be something like:

```
CheckScoresBeforeAfter() failed,
  Input:           "-5, 1, 4, -99998.7, 3"
  Expected Output: "4, 3, 1"
  Actual Output:   "1, 3, 4"
```

If this is what you want, go ahead and write it!

```
void CheckScoresBeforeAfter(...) {
    ...

    if (output != expected_output) {
        cerr << "CheckScoresBeforeAfter() failed," << endl;
        cerr << "Input:          \"" << input << "\"" << endl;
        cerr << "Expected Output: \"" << expected_output << "\"" << endl;
        cerr << "Actual Output:   \"" << output << "\"" << endl;
        abort();
    }
}
```

The moral of the story is that error messages should be as helpful as possible. Sometimes, printing your own message by building a "custom assert" is the best way to do this.

Choosing Good Test Inputs

There's an art to choosing good input values for your tests. The ones we have right now seem a bit haphazard:

```
CheckScoresBeforeAfter("-5, 1, 4, -99998.7, 3",  "4, 3, 1");
```

How do we choose good input values? Good inputs should thoroughly test the code. But they should also be simple so that they're easy to read.

> **KEY IDEA**
>
> **In general, you should pick the simplest set of inputs that completely exercise the code.**

For example, suppose we had just written:

```
CheckScoresBeforeAfter("1, 2, 3", "3, 2, 1");
```

Although this test is simple, it doesn't test the "filter negative scores" behavior of SortAndFilterDocs(). If there were a bug in that part of the code, this input wouldn't trigger it.

On the other extreme, suppose we wrote our test like this:

```
CheckScoresBeforeAfter("123014, -1082342, 823423, 234205, -235235",
                       "823423, 234205, 123014");
```

These values are needlessly complex. (And they don't even test the code thoroughly.)

Simplifying the Input Values

So what can we do to improve these input values?

```
CheckScoresBeforeAfter("-5, 1, 4, -99998.7, 3",  "4, 3, 1");
```

Well, the first thing you probably noticed is the very "loud" value -99998.7. That value was just meant to be "any negative number," so a simpler value is just -1. (If -99998.7 was meant to be "a very negative number," a better value would have been something crisp like -1e100.)

KEY IDEA
Prefer clean and simple test values that still get the job done.

The other values in our test aren't too bad, but while we're here, we can reduce them to the simplest integers possible. Also, only one negative value is needed to test that negative values are removed. Here's a new version of our test:

```
CheckScoresBeforeAfter("1, 2, -1, 3", "3, 2, 1");
```

We've simplified the test values without making them any less effective.

LARGE "SMASHER" TESTS

There is definitely value in testing your code against large, crazy inputs. For instance, you might be tempted to include a test like:

```
CheckScoresBeforeAfter("100, 38, 19, -25, 4, 84, [lots of values] ...",
                       "100, 99, 98, 97, 96, 95, 94, 93, ...");
```

Large inputs like these do a good job of exposing bugs such as buffer overruns or others you might not expect.

But code like this is big and scary to look at and not completely effective in stress-testing the code. Instead, it's more effective to construct large inputs programmatically, constructing a large input of (say) 100,000 values.

Multiple Tests of Functionality

Rather than construct a single "perfect" input to thoroughly exercise your code, it's often easier, more effective, and more readable to write multiple smaller tests.

Each test should push your code in a certain direction, trying to find a particular bug. For example, here are four tests for SortAndFilterDocs():

```
CheckScoresBeforeAfter("2, 1, 3", "3, 2, 1");     // Basic sorting
CheckScoresBeforeAfter("0, -0.1, -10", "0");      // All values < 0 removed
CheckScoresBeforeAfter("1, -2, 1, -2", "1, 1");   // Duplicates not a problem
CheckScoresBeforeAfter("", "");                   // Empty input OK
```

There are even more tests you could write if you wanted to be extremely thorough. Having separate test cases also makes it easier for the next person working on the code. If someone accidentally introduces a bug, the test failure will pinpoint the specific test that failed.

Naming Test Functions

Test code is typically organized into functions—one for each method and/or situation you're testing. For instance, the code testing SortAndFilterDocs() was inside a function named Test1():

```
void Test1() {
    ...
}
```

Picking a good name for a test function can seem tedious and irrelevant, but don't resort to meaningless names like Test1(), Test2(), and the like.

Instead, you should use the name to describe details about the test. In particular, it's handy if the person reading the test code can quickly figure out:

- The class being tested (if any)
- The function being tested
- The situation or bug being tested

A simple approach to construct a good test function name is to just concatenate that information together, possibly with a "Test_" prefix.

For instance, instead of naming it Test1(), we can use the Test_<FunctionName>() format:

```
void Test_SortAndFilterDocs() {
    ...
}
```

Depending on how sophisticated this test is, you might consider a separate test function for each situation being tested. You could use the Test_<FunctionName>_<Situation>() format:

```
void Test_SortAndFilterDocs_BasicSorting() {
    ...
}
```

```
void Test_SortAndFilterDocs_NegativeValues() {
    ...
}

...
```

Don't be afraid of having a long or clunky name here. This isn't a function that will be called throughout your codebase, so the reasons for avoiding long function names don't apply. The test function name is effectively acting like a comment. Also, if that test fails, most testing frameworks will print out the name of the function where the assertion failed, so a descriptive name is especially helpful.

Note that if you're using a testing framework, there might already be rules or conventions on how methods are named. For instance, the Python unittest module expects test method names to start with "test."

When it comes to naming *helper* functions in your test code, it's useful to highlight whether the function does any assertions itself or is just an ordinary "test-unaware" helper. For instance, in this chapter, any helper function that calls assert() is named Check...(). But the function AddScoredDoc() was named just like an ordinary helper function.

What Was Wrong with That Test?

At the beginning of the chapter, we claimed there were at least eight things wrong with this test:

```
void Test1() {
    vector<ScoredDocument> docs;
    docs.resize(5);
    docs[0].url = "http://example.com";
    docs[0].score = -5.0;
    docs[1].url = "http://example.com";
    docs[1].score = 1;
    docs[2].url = "http://example.com";
    docs[2].score = 4;
    docs[3].url = "http://example.com";
    docs[3].score = -99998.7;
    docs[4].url = "http://example.com";
    docs[4].score = 3.0;

    SortAndFilterDocs(&docs);

    assert(docs.size() == 3);
    assert(docs[0].score == 4);
    assert(docs[1].score == 3.0);
    assert(docs[2].score == 1);
}
```

Now that we've learned some techniques for writing better tests, let's identify them:

1. The test is very long and full of unimportant details. You can describe what this test is doing in one sentence, so the test statement shouldn't be much longer.

2. Adding another test isn't easy. You'd be tempted to copy/paste/modify, which would make the code even longer and full of duplication.

3. The test failure messages aren't very useful. If this test fails, it will just say `Assertion failed: docs.size() == 3`, which doesn't give you enough information to debug it further.

4. The test tries to test everything at once. It's trying to test both the negative filtering and the sorting functionality. It would be more readable to break this into multiple tests.

5. The test inputs aren't simple. In particular, the example score `-99998.7` is "loud" and gets your attention even though there isn't any significance to that specific value. A simpler negative value would suffice.

6. The test inputs don't thoroughly exercise the code. For example, it doesn't test when the score is `0`. (Would that document be filtered or not?)

7. It doesn't test other extreme inputs, such as an empty input vector, a very large vector, or one with duplicate scores.

8. The name `Test1()` is meaningless—the name should describe the function or situation being tested.

Test-Friendly Development

Some code is easier to test than other code. Ideal code to test has a well-defined interface, doesn't have much state or other "setup," and doesn't have much hidden data to inspect.

If you write your code knowing you'll be writing a test for it later, a funny thing happens: **you start designing your code so that it's easy to test!** Fortunately, coding this way also means that you create better code in general. Test-friendly designs often lead naturally to well-organized code, with separate parts to do separate things.

TEST-DRIVEN DEVELOPMENT

Test-driven development (TDD) is a programming style where you write the tests *before* you write the real code. TDD proponents believe this process profoundly improves the quality of the nontest code, much more so than if you write the tests after writing the code.

This is a hotly debated topic that we won't get into. At the very least, we've found that just keeping testing in mind while writing code helps make the code better.

But regardless of whether you employ TDD, the end result is that you have code that tests other code. The goal of this chapter is to help you make your tests easier to read and write.

Of all the ways to break up a program into classes and methods, the most decoupled ones are usually the easiest to test. On the other hand, let's say your program is very interconnected, with many method calls between your classes and lots of parameters for all the methods. Not only would that program have hard-to-understand code, but the test code would be just as ugly, and hard to read and write.

Having lots of "external" components (global variables that need to be initialized, libraries or config files that need to be loaded, etc.) also makes it more annoying to write tests.

Generally, if you're designing your code and realize, *Hmm, this is going to be a nightmare to test,* that's a good reason to stop and rethink the design. Table 14-1 shows some typical testing and design problems.

TABLE 14-1. Characteristics of less testable code, and how this leads to problems with design

Characteristic	Testability problem	Design problem
Use of global variables	All the global state needs to reset for every test (otherwise, different tests can interfere with each other).	Hard to understand which functions have what side effects. Can't think about each function in isolation; need to consider the whole program to understand if everything works.
Code depends on a lot of external components	It's harder to write any tests because there's so much scaffolding to set up first. Tests are less fun to write, so people avoid writing tests.	System is more likely to fail when one of the dependencies fails. It's harder to understand what impact any given change might make. It's harder to refactor classes. System has more failure modes and recovery paths to think about.
Code has nondeterministic behavior	Tests are flaky and unreliable. Tests that occasionally fail end up being ignored.	The program is more likely to have race conditions or other nonreproducible bugs. The program is harder to reason about. Bugs in production are very difficult to track down and fix.

On the other hand, if you have a design that's easy to write tests for, that's a good sign. Table 14-2 lists some beneficial testing and design characteristics.

TABLE 14-2. Characteristics of more testable code, and how this leads to good design

Characteristic	Testability benefit	Design benefit
Classes have little or no internal state	Tests are easier to write because there is less setup needed to test a method and less hidden state to inspect.	Classes with less state are simpler and easier to understand.
Classes/functions only do one thing	Fewer test cases are required to fully test it.	Smaller/simpler components are more modular, and the system is generally more decoupled.

Classes depend on few other classes; high decoupling	Each class can be tested independently (much easier than testing multiple classes at once).	System can be developed in parallel. Classes can be easily modified or removed without disrupting the rest of the system.
Functions have simple, well-defined interfaces	There are well-defined behaviors to test for. Simple interfaces take less work to test.	Interfaces are easier for coders to learn and are more likely to be reused.

Going Too Far

It's also possible to focus too much on testing. Here are some examples:

- **Sacrificing the readability of your real code, for the sake of enabling tests.**
  Designing your real code to be testable should be a win-win situation: your real code becomes simpler and more decoupled, and your tests are easy to write. But if you have to insert lots of ugly plumbing into your real code just so you can test it, something's wrong.

- **Being obsessive about 100% test coverage.** Testing the first 90% of your code is often less work than testing that last 10%. That last 10% might involve user interface, or dumb error cases, where the cost of the bug isn't really that high and the effort to test it just isn't worth it.

  The truth is that you'll never get 100% coverage anyhow. If it's not a missed bug, it might be a missed feature or you might not realize that the spec should be changed.

  Depending on how costly your bugs are, there's a sweet spot of how much development time it's worth spending on test code. If you're building a website prototype, it might not be worth writing any test code at all. On the other hand, if you're writing a controller for a spaceship or medical device, testing is probably your main focus.

- **Letting testing get in the way of product development.** We've seen situations where testing, which should be just one aspect of a project, dominates the whole project. Testing becomes some sort of god to be appeased, and coders just go through the rituals and motions without realizing that their precious engineering time might be better spent elsewhere.

Summary

In test code, readability is still very important. If your tests are very readable, they will in turn be very writable, so people will add more of them. Also, if you design your real code to be easy to test, your code will have a better design overall.

Here are specific points on how to improve your tests:

- The top level of each test should be as concise as possible; ideally, each test input/output can be described in one line of code.

- If your test fails, it should emit an error message that makes the bug easy to track down and fix.
- Use the simplest test inputs that completely exercise your code.
- Give your test functions a fully descriptive name so it's clear what each is testing. Instead of Test1(), use a name like Test_<FunctionName>_<Situation>.

And above all, make it easy to modify and add new tests.

## CHAPTER FIFTEEN

Designing and Implementing a "Minute/Hour Counter"

Let's take a look at a data structure used in real production code: a "minute/hour counter." We'll take you through the natural thought process an engineer might go through, first trying to solve this problem and then improving its performance and adding features. Most important, we'll also be trying to keep the code easy to read, using principles from throughout this book. We might take some wrong turns along the way or make other mistakes. See if you can follow along and catch them.

The Problem

We need to keep track of how many bytes a web server has transferred over the past minute and over the past hour. Here's an illustration of how these totals are maintained:

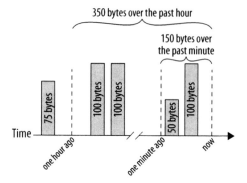

It's a fairly straightforward problem, but as you'll see, solving it efficiently is an interesting challenge. Let's start by defining the class interface.

Defining the Class Interface

Here is our first version of the class interface in C++:

```
class MinuteHourCounter {
  public:
    // Add a count
    void Count(int num_bytes);

    // Return the count over this minute
    int MinuteCount();

    // Return the count over this hour
    int HourCount();
};
```

Before we implement this class, let's go through the names and comments to see if there's anything we want to change.

Improving the Names

The class name `MinuteHourCounter` is pretty good. It's very specific, concrete, and easy to say.

Given the class name, the method names `MinuteCount()` and `HourCount()` are also reasonable. You might have called them `GetMinuteCount()` and `GetHourCount()`, but this doesn't help anything. As we said in Chapter 3, *Names That Can't Be Misconstrued*, "get" implies "lightweight accessor" to many people. And as you'll see, the implementation won't be lightweight, so it's best to leave "get" out.

The method name `Count()` is problematic, though. We asked our coworkers what they thought `Count()` would do, and some thought it meant "return the total number of counts over all time." The name is a bit counterintuitive (no pun intended). The problem is that `Count` is both a noun and a verb and could mean either "I want a count of the number of samples you have seen" or "I want you to count this sample."

Here are alternative names to consider in place of `Count()`:

- `Increment()`
- `Observe()`
- `Record()`
- `Add()`

`Increment()` is misleading because it implies that there's a value that only increases. (In our case, the hour count fluctuates over time.)

`Observe()` is okay, but a little vague.

`Record()` also has the noun/verb problem, so that's no good.

`Add()` is interesting because it can either mean "add this numerically" or "add to a list of data"—in our case, it's a little of both, so that works. So we'll rename the method to `void Add(int num_bytes)`.

But the argument name `num_bytes` is too specific. Yes, our primary use case is for counting bytes, but `MinuteHourCounter` doesn't need to know this. Someone else might use this class to count queries or database transactions. We could use a more generic name like `delta`, but the term `delta` is often used in places where the value can be negative, which we don't want. The name `count` should work—it's simple, generic, and implies "nonnegative." Also, it lets us sneak in the word "count" in a less ambiguous context.

Improving the Comments

Here's the class interface we have so far:

```
class MinuteHourCounter {
  public:
```

```
    // Add a count
    void Add(int count);

    // Return the count over this minute
    int MinuteCount();

    // Return the count over this hour
    int HourCount();
};
```

Let's go through each of these method comments and improve them. Consider the first one:

```
    // Add a count
    void Add(int count);
```

This comment is completely redundant now—it should be either removed or improved. Here's an improved version:

```
    // Add a new data point (count >= 0).
    // For the next minute, MinuteCount() will be larger by +count.
    // For the next hour, HourCount() will be larger by +count.
    void Add(int count);
```

Now let's consider the comment for MinuteCount():

```
    // Return the count over this minute
    int MinuteCount();
```

When we asked our coworkers what this comment meant, there were two conflicting interpretations:

1. Return the count during this current clock-minute, such as 12:13 p.m.

2. Return the count during the past 60 seconds, regardless of clock-minute boundaries.

The second interpretation is how it actually works. So let's clear up this confusion with language that is more precise and detailed:

```
    // Return the accumulated count over the past 60 seconds.
    int MinuteCount();
```

(Similarly, we should improve the comment for HourCount().)

Here is the class definition with all the changes so far, along with a class-level comment:

```
    // Track the cumulative counts over the past minute and over the past hour.
    // Useful, for example, to track recent bandwidth usage.
    class MinuteHourCounter {
        // Add a new data point (count >= 0).
        // For the next minute, MinuteCount() will be larger by +count.
        // For the next hour, HourCount() will be larger by +count.
        void Add(int count);

        // Return the accumulated count over the past 60 seconds.
        int MinuteCount();
```

```
// Return the accumulated count over the past 3600 seconds.
int HourCount();
};
```

(For brevity, we'll leave the comments out of the code listings from now on.)

GETTING AN OUTSIDE PERSPECTIVE

You may have noticed that there were already a couple cases where we ran things by our coworkers. Asking for an outside perspective is a great way to test if your code is "user-friendly." Try to be open to their first impressions, because other people may come to the same conclusions. And those "other people" may include *you* in six months.

Attempt 1: A Naive Solution

Let's move on to solving the problem. We'll start with a straightforward solution: just keep a list of timestamped "events":

```
class MinuteHourCounter {
    struct Event {
        Event(int count, time_t time) : count(count), time(time) {}
        int count;
        time_t time;
    };

    list<Event> events;

  public:
    void Add(int count) {
        events.push_back(Event(count, time()));
    }

    ...
};
```

We can then count over the most recent events as needed:

```
class MinuteHourCounter {
    ...

    int MinuteCount() {
        int count = 0;
        const time_t now_secs = time();
        for (list<Event>::reverse_iterator i = events.rbegin();
             i != events.rend() && i->time > now_secs - 60; ++i) {
            count += i->count;
        }
        return count;
    }
```

```
    int HourCount() {
        int count = 0;
        const time_t now_secs = time();
        for (list<Event>::reverse_iterator i = events.rbegin();
            i != events.rend() && i->time > now_secs - 3600; ++i) {
            count += i->count;
        }
        return count;
    }
};
```

Is the Code Easy to Understand?

Although this solution is "correct," there are a couple readability problems:

- **The for loops are a bit of a mouthful.** Most readers slow down significantly while they're reading this part of the code (at least they should, if they're making sure there aren't any bugs).

- **MinuteCount() and HourCount() are almost identical.** It would make the code smaller if they could share the duplicated code. This detail is especially important because the redundant code is relatively complex. (Better to have all the difficult code confined to one place.)

An Easier-to-Read Version

The code for MinuteCount() and HourCount() differs by only a single constant (60 vs. 3600). The obvious refactoring is to introduce a helper method to handle both cases:

```
class MinuteHourCounter {
    list<Event> events;

    int CountSince(time_t cutoff) {
        int count = 0;
        for (list<Event>::reverse_iterator rit = events.rbegin();
            rit != events.rend(); ++rit) {
            if (rit->time <= cutoff) {
                break;
            }
            count += rit->count;
        }
        return count;
    }

public:
    void Add(int count) {
        events.push_back(Event(count, time()));
    }

    int MinuteCount() {
        return CountSince(time() - 60);
```

```
        }

        int HourCount() {
            return CountSince(time() - 3600);
        }
};
```

There are a few things worth pointing out about this new code.

First, notice that CountSince() takes an absolute cutoff parameter, rather than a relative secs_ago value (60 or 3600). Either way would have worked, but this way CountSince() has a slightly easier job to do.

Second, we renamed the iterator from i to rit. The name i is more commonly used for integer indexes. We contemplated using the name it, which is typical for iterators. But in this case we have a *reverse* iterator, and this fact is crucial to the correctness of the code. By having a variable name prefixed with r, it adds a comforting symmetry to statements like rit != events.rend().

Finally, we extracted the condition rit->time <= cutoff out of the for loop, and made it a separate if statement. Why? Because "traditional" for loops of the form for(begin; end; advance) are easiest to read. The reader can immediately understand it as "go through all the elements" and doesn't have to think about it further.

Performance Problems

Although we've improved how the code looks, this design has two serious performance problems:

1. **It just keeps growing and growing.**

   The class holds on to all of the events it's ever seen—it uses an unbounded amount of memory! Ideally, the MinuteHourCounter should automatically delete events that are older than an hour because they're no longer needed.

2. **MinuteCount() and HourCount() are too slow.**

   The method CountSince() takes *O(n)* time, where *n* is the number of data points in the relevant time window. Imagine a high-performance server that called Add() hundreds of times per second. Every call to HourCount() would have to count through a million data points! Ideally, the MinuteHourCounter should keep separate minute_count and hour_count variables that are kept up date with each call to Add().

Attempt 2: Conveyor Belt Design

We need a design that solves both of the previous problems:

1. Delete data we no longer need.

2. Keep precomputed minute_count and hour_count totals up to date.

Here's how we'll do it: we'll use our list like a conveyor belt. When new data arrives on one end, we add to our total. And when the data is too old, it "falls off" the other end, and we subtract from our total.

There are a couple ways we could implement this conveyor belt design. One way is to maintain two independent lists, one for events in the past minute, one for those in the past hour. When a new event comes in, add a copy to both lists.

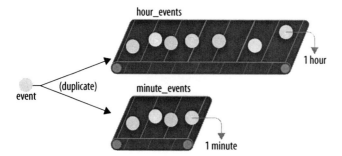

This way is pretty simple, but it's inefficient because it makes two copies of every event.

Another way is to maintain two lists, where events initially go into the first list (the "last minute events"), and then this feeds into the second list (the "last hour [but not last minute] events").

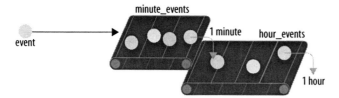

This "two-stage" conveyor belt design seems more efficient, so let's implement this one.

Implementing the Two-Stage Conveyor Belt Design

Let's begin by listing the members of our class:

```
class MinuteHourCounter {
    list<Event> minute_events;
    list<Event> hour_events;  // only contains elements NOT in minute_events

    int minute_count;
    int hour_count;  // counts ALL events over past hour, including past minute
};
```

The crux of this conveyor belt design is to be able to "shift" the events as time goes by, so that events move from minute_events to hour_events, and minute_count and hour_count get updated accordingly. To do this, we'll create a helper method named ShiftOldEvents(). Once we have that method, the rest of the class is fairly easy to implement:

```cpp
void Add(int count) {
    const time_t now_secs = time();
    ShiftOldEvents(now_secs);

    // Feed into the minute list (not into the hour list--that will happen later)
    minute_events.push_back(Event(count, now_secs));

    minute_count += count;
    hour_count += count;
}

int MinuteCount() {
    ShiftOldEvents(time());
    return minute_count;
}

int HourCount() {
    ShiftOldEvents(time());
    return hour_count;
}
```

Clearly, we've deferred all the dirty work to ShiftOldEvents():

```cpp
// Find and delete old events, and decrease hour_count and minute_count accordingly.
void ShiftOldEvents(time_t now_secs) {
    const int minute_ago = now_secs - 60;
    const int hour_ago = now_secs - 3600;

    // Move events more than one minute old from 'minute_events' into 'hour_events'
    // (Events older than one hour will be removed in the second loop.)
    while (!minute_events.empty() && minute_events.front().time <= minute_ago) {
        hour_events.push_back(minute_events.front());

        minute_count -= minute_events.front().count;
        minute_events.pop_front();
    }

    // Remove events more than one hour old from 'hour_events'
    while (!hour_events.empty() && hour_events.front().time <= hour_ago) {
        hour_count -= hour_events.front().count;
        hour_events.pop_front();
    }
}
```

Are We Done?

We've solved the two performance concerns we mentioned earlier, and our solution works. For many applications, this solution would be good enough. But there are a number of deficiencies, too.

First, the design is very inflexible. Suppose we wanted to keep counts over the past 24 hours. That would require making a lot of changes to the code. And as you probably noticed, ShiftOldEvents() is a pretty dense function, with subtle interaction between the minute and hour data.

Second, this class has a pretty big memory footprint. Suppose you had a high-traffic server calling Add() 100 times per second. Because we hold on to all data over the past hour, this code would end up requiring about 5MB of memory.

In general, the more frequently Add() is called, the more memory we use. In a production environment, libraries that use a large, unpredictable amount of memory aren't good. Ideally, the MinuteHourCounter would use a fixed amount of memory no matter how often Add() is called.

Attempt 3: A Time-Bucketed Design

You may not have noticed, but both of the previous implementations had a small bug. We used time_t to store the timestamp, which stores an integral number of seconds. Because of this rounding, MinuteCount() actually returns somewhere between 59 and 60 seconds worth of data, depending on when exactly you call it.

For example, if an event happens at time = 0.99 seconds, that time will get rounded to t=0 seconds. And if you call MinuteCount() at time = 60.1 seconds, it will return the total for events where t=1,2,3,...60. So that first event will be missed, even though it's technically less than a minute ago.

On average, MinuteCount() will return 59.5 seconds worth of data. And HourCount() will return 3599.5 seconds worth of data (a negligible error).

We could fix all this by using a time with subsecond granularity. But interestingly, most applications using a MinuteHourCounter don't need that level of accuracy in the first place. We will exploit this fact to design a new MinuteHourCounter that's much faster and uses less space. It's a trade-off of precision for performance that will be well worth it.

The key idea is to *bucket* all the events within a small time window together, and summarize those events with a single total. For instance, the events over the past minute could be inserted into 60 discrete buckets, each 1 second wide. The events over the past hour could also be inserted into 60 discrete buckets, each 1 minute wide.

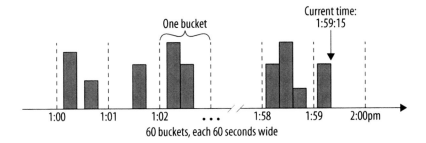

Using the buckets as shown, the methods MinuteCount() and HourCount() will be accurate to 1 part per 60, which is reasonable.*

If more precision is needed, more buckets can be used in exchange for a larger memory footprint. But the important thing is that this design has a fixed, predictable memory usage.

Implementing the Time-Bucketed Design

Implementing this design with just one class would create a lot of intricate code that's hard to wrap your head around. Instead, we're going to follow our advice from Chapter 11, *One Task at a Time*, and create separate classes to handle the different parts of this problem.

For starters, let's create a separate class to keep track of the counts for a single time span (like the last hour). We'll call it a TrailingBucketCounter. It's essentially a generic version of MinuteHourCounter that handles only one time span. Here's the interface:

```
// A class that keeps counts for the past N buckets of time.
class TrailingBucketCounter {
  public:
    // Example: TrailingBucketCounter(30, 60) tracks the last 30 minute-buckets of time.
    TrailingBucketCounter(int num_buckets, int secs_per_bucket);

    void Add(int count, time_t now);

    // Return the total count over the last num_buckets worth of time
    int TrailingCount(time_t now);
};
```

You might wonder why Add() and TrailingCount() require the current time (time_t now) as an argument—wouldn't it be easier if those methods just computed the current time() themselves?

---

* Similar to the previous solutions, the last bucket will be only half-full on average. With this design, we could remedy the underestimate by keeping 61 buckets instead of 60 and ignoring the current "in-progress" bucket. But this causes the data to be partially "stale." A better fix is to combine the in-progress bucket with a complementary fraction of the oldest bucket to obtain a count that is both unbiased and up to date. This implementation is left as an exercise for the reader.

Although it may seem strange, passing in the current time has a couple benefits. First, it makes TrailingBucketCounter a "clockless" class, which in general is easier to test and less bug-prone. Second, it keeps all the calls to time() inside MinuteHourCounter. With time-sensitive systems, it helps if you can put all the calls to get the time in one place.

Assuming TrailingBucketCounter was already implemented, the MinuteHourCounter is easy to implement:

```cpp
class MinuteHourCounter {
    TrailingBucketCounter minute_counts;
    TrailingBucketCounter hour_counts;

  public:
    MinuteHourCounter() :
        minute_counts(/* num_buckets = */ 60, /* secs_per_bucket = */ 1),
        hour_counts(  /* num_buckets = */ 60, /* secs_per_bucket = */ 60) {
    }

    void Add(int count) {
        time_t now = time();
        minute_counts.Add(count, now);
        hour_counts.Add(count, now);
    }

    int MinuteCount() {
        time_t now = time();
        return minute_counts.TrailingCount(now);
    }

    int HourCount() {
        time_t now = time();
        return hour_counts.TrailingCount(now);
    }
};
```

This code is much more readable, and also more flexible—if we wanted to increase the number of buckets (to improve precision but increase memory usage), that would be easy to do.

Implementing TrailingBucketCounter

Now all that's left is to implement the TrailingBucketCounter class. Once again, we're going to create a helper class to break down this problem further.

We'll create a data structure called ConveyorQueue whose job is to deal with the underlying counts and their totals. The TrailingBucketCounter class can focus on the task of moving the ConveyorQueue according to how much time has elapsed.

Here is the ConveyorQueue interface:

```cpp
// A queue with a maximum number of slots, where old data "falls off" the end.
class ConveyorQueue {
    ConveyorQueue(int max_items);
```

```
    // Increment the value at the back of the queue.
    void AddToBack(int count);

    // Each value in the queue is shifted forward by 'num_shifted'.
    // New items are initialized to 0.
    // Oldest items will be removed so there are <= max_items.
    void Shift(int num_shifted);

    // Return the total value of all items currently in the queue.
    int TotalSum();
};
```

Assuming this class was implemented, look how easy the TrailingBucketCounter is to implement:

```
class TrailingBucketCounter {
    ConveyorQueue buckets;
    const int secs_per_bucket;
    time_t last_update_time;  // the last time Update() was called

    // Calculate how many buckets of time have passed and Shift() accordingly.
    void Update(time_t now) {
        int current_bucket = now / secs_per_bucket;
        int last_update_bucket = last_update_time / secs_per_bucket;

        buckets.Shift(current_bucket - last_update_bucket);
        last_update_time = now;
    }

  public:
    TrailingBucketCounter(int num_buckets, int secs_per_bucket) :
        buckets(num_buckets),
        secs_per_bucket(secs_per_bucket) {
    }

    void Add(int count, time_t now) {
        Update(now);
        buckets.AddToBack(count);
    }

    int TrailingCount(time_t now) {
        Update(now);
        return buckets.TotalSum();
    }
};
```

This breakdown into two classes (TrailingBucketCounter and ConveyorQueue) is another instance of what we discussed in Chapter 11, *One Task at a Time*. We could also have done without ConveyorQueue and implemented everything directly inside TrailingBucketCounter. But this way, the code is easier to digest.

Implementing ConveyorQueue

Now all that's left is to implement the ConveyorQueue class:

```cpp
// A queue with a maximum number of slots, where old data gets shifted off the end.
class ConveyorQueue {
    queue<int> q;
    int max_items;
    int total_sum;  // sum of all items in q

  public:
    ConveyorQueue(int max_items) : max_items(max_items), total_sum(0) {
    }

    int TotalSum() {
        return total_sum;
    }

    void Shift(int num_shifted) {
        // In case too many items shifted, just clear the queue.
        if (num_shifted >= max_items) {
            q = queue<int>();  // clear the queue
            total_sum = 0;
            return;
        }

        // Push all the needed zeros.
        while (num_shifted > 0) {
            q.push(0);
            num_shifted--;
        }

        // Let all the excess items fall off.
        while (q.size() > max_items) {
            total_sum -= q.front();
            q.pop();
        }
    }

    void AddToBack(int count) {
        if (q.empty()) Shift(1);  // Make sure q has at least 1 item.
        q.back() += count;
        total_sum += count;
    }
};
```

Now we're done! We have a MinuteHourCounter that's fast and memory-efficient, plus a more flexible TrailingBucketCounter that's easily reusable. For instance, it would be pretty easy to create a more versatile RecentCounter that can count a wide range of intervals, such as the last day or last ten minutes.

Comparing the Three Solutions

Let's compare the solutions we've looked at in this chapter. The following table shows the code size and performance stats (assuming a high-traffic use case of 100 Add()/sec):

Solution	Lines of code	Cost per HourCount()	Memory use	Error in HourCount()
Naive solution	33	O(#events-per-hour) (~3.6 million)	unbounded	1 part per 3600
Conveyor belt design	55	O(1)	O(#events-per-hour) (~5MB)	1 part per 3600
Time-bucketed design (60 buckets)	98	O(1)	O(#buckets) (~500 bytes)	1 part per 60

Notice that the total amount of code for our final three-class solution is more than for any of the other attempts. However, the performance is far superior, and the design is more flexible. Also, each class individually is much easier to read. This is always a positive change: having 100 lines that are all easy to read is better than 50 lines that aren't.

Sometimes, breaking a problem into multiple classes can introduce interclass complexity (that a one-class solution wouldn't have). In this case, though, there's a simple "linear" chain of use from one class to the next, and only one of the classes is exposed to end users. Overall, the benefits of breaking this problem down make this a win.

Summary

Let's review the steps we went through to get to the final MinuteHourCounter design. The process is typical of how other pieces of code evolve.

First, we started by coding a naive solution. This helped us realize two design challenges: speed and memory use.

Next, we tried a "conveyor belt" design. This design improved the speed and memory use but still wasn't good enough for high-performance applications. Also, this design was very inflexible: adapting the code to handle other time intervals would be a lot of work.

Our final design solved the previous problems by breaking things down into subproblems. Here are the three classes we created, in bottom-up order, and the subproblem each one solved:

ConveyorQueue

A maximum-length queue that can be "shifted" and maintains its total sum

TrailingBucketCounter

Moves the ConveyorQueue according to how much time has elapsed and maintains the count of a single (latest) time interval, with a given precision

MinuteHourCounter

Simply contains two TrailingBucketCounters, one for the minute count and one for the hour count

Further Reading

We created this book by analyzing hundreds of code examples from production code to figure out what works in practice. But we've also read many books and articles that helped us in this pursuit.

If you're interested in learning more, here are some resources you might like. The following lists are by no means complete, but they're a good place to start.

Books on Writing High-Quality Code

Code Complete: A Practical Handbook of Software Construction, 2nd edition, by Steve McConnell (Microsoft Press, 2004)
> A rigorous and well-researched tome on all aspects of software construction, including code quality and more.

Refactoring: Improving the Design of Existing Code, by Martin Fowler et al. (Addison-Wesley Professional, 1999)
> A great book that talks about the philosophy of incremental code improvements and contains a detailed catalog of many different refactorings, along with steps to take to make these changes with less chance of breaking things.

The Practice of Programming, by Brian Kernighan and Rob Pike (Addison-Wesley Professional, 1999)
> Discusses various aspects of programming including debugging, testing, portability, and performance, with various coding examples.

The Pragmatic Programmer: From Journeyman to Master, by Andrew Hunt and David Thomas (Addison-Wesley Professional, 1999)
> A collection of many good programming and engineering principles, organized into short discussions.

Clean Code: A Handbook of Agile Software Craftsmanship, by Robert C. Martin (Prentice Hall, 2008)
> A book similar to ours (but Java-specific); explores other topics such as error handling and concurrency.

Books on Various Programming Topics

JavaScript: The Good Parts, by Douglas Crockford (O'Reilly, 2008)
> We believe this book has a similar spirit to ours, even though the book isn't explicitly about readability. It's about using a clean subset of the JavaScript language that is less error-prone and easier to reason about.

Effective Java, 2nd edition, by Joshua Bloch (Prentice Hall, 2008)
> A phenomenal book about making your Java programs easier to read and more bug-free. Although it's about Java, many of the principles apply to all languages. Highly recommended.

Design Patterns: Elements of Reusable Object-Oriented Software, by Erich Gamma, Richard Helm, Ralph Johnson, and John Vlissides (Addison-Wesley Professional, 1994)

> The original book on a common language of "patterns" for software engineers to talk about object-oriented programming. As a catalog of common, useful patterns, it helps programmers avoid the pitfalls that often happen when people try to solve a tricky problem on their own for the first time.

Programming Pearls, 2nd edition, by Jon Bentley (Addison-Wesley Professional, 1999)

> A series of articles on real software problems. Great insights on solving real-world problems in each chapter.

High Performance Web Sites, by Steve Souders (O'Reilly, 2007)

> Although not a book about programming, this book is noteworthy because it describes a number of ways to optimize a website without writing much code (in keeping with Chapter 13, *Writing Less Code*).

Joel on Software: And on Diverse and …, by Joel Spolsky

> Some of the best articles from *http://www.joelonsoftware.com/*. Spolsky writes about many aspects of software engineering and has an insightful take on many related topics. Be sure to read "Things You Should Never Do, Part I," and "The Joel Test: 12 Steps to Better Code."

Books of Historical Note

Writing Solid Code, by Steve Maguire (Microsoft Press, 1993)

> This book has unfortunately become a bit dated, but it definitely influenced us with great advice about how to make your code more bug-free. If you read it, you'll notice a lot of overlap with what we recommend.

Smalltalk Best Practice Patterns, by Kent Beck (Prentice Hall, 1996)

> Although the examples are in Smalltalk, the book has many good programming principles.

The Elements of Programming Style, by Brian Kernighan and P.J. Plauger (Computing McGraw-Hill, 1978)

> One of the oldest books dealing with the issue of "the clearest way to write things." Most of the examples are in Fortran and PL1.

Literate Programming, by Donald E. Knuth (Center for the Study of Language and Information, 1992)

> We agree wholeheartedly with Knuth's statement, "Instead of imagining that our main task is to instruct a *computer* what to do, let us concentrate rather on explaining to *human beings* what we want a computer to do" (p. 99). But be warned: the bulk of the book is about Knuth's WEB programming environment for documentation. WEB is effectively a language for writing your programs as works of literature, with code on the sidelines.

Having used a WEB-derived system ourselves, we think that when code is constantly changing (which is usually), it's harder to keep a so-called "literate program" fresh than it is to keep your code fresh using the practices we recommend.

Symbols

We'd like to hear your suggestions for improving our indexes. Send email to *index@oreilly.com*.

clever code, confusion from, 86
Clip() function, 24
closure in JavaScript, 99
code, viii, 150
    (see also test code)
    eliminating duplicate, 38
    isolating regions of, 129
    less vs. more, 3
    multiple tasks vs. single, 122–130
    qualities of good, 2
    redundant, 170
    removing unused, 143
    test-friendly development, 160
    turning thoughts into, 132–138
    understandable, 2
    writing less, 140–145
codebases
    directory for general-purpose code, 114
    keeping small, 142
column alignment, 38–39
command-line flag, name for, 14
comments, 3, 46–57, 60–65
    ambiguous pronouns in, 60
    big picture, 54
    code flaw descriptions, 50–51
    compactness, 60
    constants explained, 51
    function behavior description, 61
    information-dense words in, 64
    input/output examples to illustrate corner
        cases, 61–62
    insights about code in, 50
    intent statement for code, 62–63
    lining up, 36–37
    minute/hour counter improvements, 167–169
    named function parameter, 63–64
    names and, 49
    preciseness, 60, 61
    purpose of, 46
    reader's perspective for, 51
    summary, 42, 55
    what, why, or how, 56
    when not to use, 47–49
    writer's block, 56
complex idea, ability to explain, 132
complexity, 142
complicated logic, breaking down, 86–88
concrete names, vs. abstract, 13–15
conditional expression (?:), 73–74
conditionals, order of arguments, 70
consistent layout, 34
    line breaks for, 35–37
    personal style vs., 42
constants, 103
    comments to explain, 51

constructors, formatting names, 21
continue statement, 75
control flow, 70–81
    ?: conditional expression, 73–74
    early return from function, 75–76
    eliminating variables, 96
    following flow of execution, 80
    goto statement, 76
    nesting, 77–79
ConveyorQueue interface, 176
    implementing, 178
cookies in JavaScript, 116
copy constructor, default, 13
corner cases, input/output comment examples to
        illustrate, 61–62
crutch comments, 49

D

dashes, names with, 20
database tables, program to join, 134–137
De Morgan's laws, 85
declarations, organized into blocks, 40–41
defragmenting code, 122
deleting unused code, 143
design, vs. aesthetics, 34
development time, sweet spot for, 162
dictionary in Python, 144
    sensitive information in, 117
DISALLOW_COPY_AND_ASSIGN macro, 14
DISALLOW_EVIL_CONSTRUCTOR macro, 13
do-while loops, avoiding, 74–75
DRY (Don't Repeat Yourself) principle, 89
duplicated code, eliminating, 38

E

Eclipse, word-completion command, 19
Emacs, word-completion command, 19
end, inclusive/exclusive ranges using, 26–27
error messages
    hand-crafted, 155–156
    readability, 154–156
exceptions, 80
execution flow, following, 80
expectations of users, matching, 27–28
explaining variables, 84
expressions
    breaking down, 84–91
    complicated logic in, 86–88
    one-line vs. multiple lines, 3
    short-circuit logic abuse, 86
    simplifying, 90
external components
    testing issues, 161
extracting, 110

(see also subproblems code extraction)
values from object, 124–128

F

false, 27
features, decision not to implement, 140
file contents, reading, 112
Filter() function, 24
findClosestLocation() example, 110–111
first and last, inclusive ranges using, 26
FIXME: marker, 50
flow of execution, following, 80
for loops, 170, 171
    removing nesting inside, 78–79
formatting names, meaning from, 20–21
format_pretty() function, 113
Fowler, Martin, Refactoring: Improving the Design
    of Existing Code, 119
function pointers, 80
functionality, project-specific, 115
functions
    anonymous, 80
    comments for behavior description, 61
    early return from, 75–76, 78
    extracting code into separate, 110–118
    names of, 8
    wrapper, 116
fundamental theory of readability, 3

G

general-purpose code, 112–114
    creating, 114
generic names, 10–12
get*() methods, user expectations for, 27
global scope, JavaScript, 100
global variables
    avoiding, 97
    testability, 161
Google
    DISALLOW_EVIL_CONSTRUCTOR macro, 14
    formatting conventions for open-source
        projects, 20–21
Gosling, James, 104
goto statement, 76

H

HACK: marker, 50
helper methods, 37, 130
    names in test code, 159
    ShiftOldEvents() in minute/hour counter, 173
    test code clean-up with, 151
high-level comments, 55
HTML tags, id or class attribute names, 21
HttpDownload object, 128

Hungarian notation, 17

I

if statement
    assignment inside, 71
    handling separate, 127–128
    name of index for, 12
    order of arguments, 70
    scope in C++, 98
if/else blocks, order of, 72–73
immutable data types, 104
implementing features, decision not to, 140
inclusive ranges, first and last for, 26
inclusive/exclusive ranges, begin and end for, 26–
    27
indices, names for, 12
information-dense words, comments with, 64
inline comments, named function parameters in,
    64
input values, choosing good for test, 156–158
input/output comment examples, to illustrate
    corner cases, 61–62
IntelliJ IDEA, word-completion command, 19
interface
    reshaping, 117
    simplifying existing, 116
intermediate result variable, eliminating, 95, 101,
    105
isolating regions of code, 129

J

Java
    block scope, 100–101
    inline comment for named function parameter,
        64
    structured idiom for cleanup code, 76
JavaScript
    alert(), 112
    cookies, 116
    findClosestLocation() example, 110–111
    formatting names, 21
    function to remove value from array, 95
    global scope, 100
    no nested scope, 100–101
    or operator, 86
    private variables in, 99
jQuery JavaScript library, 133
jQuery library function, formatting names, 21

L

last, inclusive ranges using, 26
libraries, 116
    knowledge of, 133–134, 143–144
    regular expressions, 153

R

ranges
    inclusive, first and last for, 26
    inclusive/exclusive, begin and end for, 26–27
readability
    error messages and, 154–156
    fundamental theory of, 3
    test code and, 150–153
    variables and, 94–106
reading file contents, 112
redundancy check, comment as, 63
redundant code, 170
Refactoring: Improving the Design of Existing Code
    (Fowler), 119
regular expressions
    libraries, 153
    precompiling, 115
removing unused code, 143
requirements, questions and breakdown, 140–141
return value, name for, 10
returning early from function, 75–76
    removing nesting by, 78
reverse iterator, 171
Ruby, or operator, 86
--run locally command-line flag, 14–15

S

scope
    global, in JavaScript, 100
    if statement in C++, 98
    name length and, 18
    of variables, shrinking, 97–102
security bug, names and, 17
sets in Python, 144
ShiftOldEvents() method, 173
short-circuit logic abuse, 86
signal/interrupt handlers, 80
silhouette of code, 36
Smalltalk Best Practice Patterns (Beck), 119
specificity of words, name selection and, 8–10
statements, breaking down, 89
static methods, 98
statistics, incrementing, 128–130
stock purchases, recording, 134–137
store locator for business, 140–141
Stroustrup, Bjarne, 75
subproblems code extraction, 110–118
    findClosestLocation() example, 110–111
    general-purpose code, 112–114
    project-specific functionality, 115
    simplifying existing interface, 116
    taking things too far, 117
    utility code, 111–112
summary comments, 42, 55

summary variables, 84–85, 89
"surface-level" improvements, 5

T

tasks
    extracting values from object, 124–128
    multiple vs. single, 122–130
    size of, 123–124
    UpdateCounts() function example, 128–130
temporary variables, 94
ternary operator, 73–74
test code
    creating minimal statement, 152
    helper method names in, 159
    locating problems in, 150
    readability, 150–153
Test-Driven Development (TDD), 160
testing, 150–163
    CheckScoresBeforeAfter() function for, 153
    choosing good input values, 156–158
    code development and, 160
    going too far, 162
    and good design, 161
    identifying problems in, 159–160
    large inputs for, 157
    multiple tests of functionality, 158
    names for test functions, 158–159
    website changes, 29
text editors, word-completion command, 19
TextMate, word-completion command, 19
threading, 80
time, requirement for understanding code, 3
time-sensitive systems, 176
tmp variable, alternative, 11
TODO: marker, 50
top-down programming, 114
TrailingBucketCounter class, 176–177
true, 27
typo, column alignment to find, 39

U

underscores, names with, 20
Unix tools, 144
UpdateCounts() function, 128–130
user authorization for web page, PHP for, 132
user information, Python dictionary with sensitive,
    117
users, matching expectations, 27–28
utility code, extracting, 111–112

V

values, extracting from object, 124–128
var keyword (JavaScript), 100
variables

Although raised in the circus, **Dustin Boswell** realized early on that he was better at computers than at acrobatics. Dustin received his B.S. from Caltech, where he got hooked on computer science, and then went to UC San Diego for his master's degree. He worked at Google for five years, on a variety of projects including web crawling infrastructure. He's built numerous websites and enjoys working on "big data" and machine learning. Dustin is now an Internet startup junkie who spends his free time hiking the Santa Monica mountains and being a new dad.

Trevor Foucher has worked on large-scale software development at Microsoft and Google for over 10 years. He is currently an engineer on search infrastructure at Google. In his spare time, he attends gaming conventions, reads science fiction, and serves as COO of his wife's fashion start-up company. Trevor graduated with a BS degree in Electrical Engineering and Computer Science from UC Berkeley.

COLOPHON

The cover image is from Getty Images. The cover fonts are Akzidenz Grotesk and Orator. The text font is Adobe's Meridien; the heading font is ITC Bailey.

Get even more for your money.

Join the O'Reilly Community, and register the O'Reilly books you own. It's free, and you'll get:

- $4.99 ebook upgrade offer
- 40% upgrade offer on O'Reilly print books
- Membership discounts on books and events
- Free lifetime updates to ebooks and videos
- Multiple ebook formats, DRM FREE
- Participation in the O'Reilly community
- Newsletters
- Account management
- 100% Satisfaction Guarantee

Signing up is easy:

1. **Go to: oreilly.com/go/register**
2. **Create an O'Reilly login.**
3. **Provide your address.**
4. **Register your books.**

Note: English-language books only

To order books online:
oreilly.com/store

For questions about products or an order:
orders@oreilly.com

To sign up to get topic-specific email announcements and/or news about upcoming books, conferences, special offers, and new technologies:
elists@oreilly.com

For technical questions about book content:
booktech@oreilly.com

To submit new book proposals to our editors:
proposals@oreilly.com

O'Reilly books are available in multiple DRM-free ebook formats. For more information:
oreilly.com/ebooks

O'REILLY®

Spreading the knowledge of innovators   oreilly.com

The information you need, when and where you need it.

With Safari Books Online, you can:

Access the contents of thousands of technology and business books

- Quickly search over 7000 books and certification guides
- Download whole books or chapters in PDF format, at no extra cost, to print or read on the go
- Copy and paste code
- Save up to 35% on O'Reilly print books
- **New!** Access mobile-friendly books directly from cell phones and mobile devices

Stay up-to-date on emerging topics before the books are published

- Get on-demand access to evolving manuscripts.
- Interact directly with authors of upcoming books

Explore thousands of hours of video on technology and design topics

- Learn from expert video tutorials
- Watch and replay recorded conference sessions

CPSIA information can be obtained at www.ICGtesting.com
Printed in the USA
LVOW11s2006160913

352678LV00017B/1170/P